AF504516

A Union Without Division

Where Unity Reflects God's Glory

DARRELL CANTY

The Mitchelle

8230 Wilbarn St., Paramount, CA 90723

(323) 986-5847

Copyright © 2026 Darrell Canty. All rights reserved.

No part of this book may be reproduced, stored in a retrieval system, or transmitted by any means without the written permission of the author.

Published by The Mitchelle

Paperback: 979-8-89668-000-0
eBook: 979-8-89668-001-7

Any people depicted in stock imagery provided by Shutterstock are models, and such images are being used for illustrative purposes only.

Certain stock imagery © Shutterstock

Because of the dynamic nature of the Internet, any web addresses or links contained in this book may have changed since publication and may no longer be valid. The views expressed in this work are solely those of the author and do not necessarily reflect the views of the publisher, and the publisher hereby disclaims any responsibility for them.

Dedication

A Special dedication to Ken & Pondra Canty—for a marriage that's forged on the desires to please God, with their marriage and in their marriage.

This dedication is for all those who yearn for a truly Godly marriage, who seek the union designed by the Creator, grounded in His truth, love, and unwavering faithfulness. It is for those who have endured the trials of a marriage built on false pretenses, where promises were empty, and God's light was dimmed by deception. It is for those who married someone who claimed a godly heart but revealed otherwise—this is for you. Know that your pain and tears were not unseen, and the God who understands every sorrow holds you closely, offering healing and a renewed hope.

This book is also for those who may have been the ones who misled others. Whether through a journey of brokenness, misunderstanding, or dishonesty, know that God's grace is deep enough to redeem and transform. For those willing to change, there is hope and forgiveness that can lead to a new path—one where godliness is genuine, and love is unselfish.

To those who feel defeated, disillusioned, or ready to give up on finding a marriage without division, take heart. With God, it is possible to experience a love that reflects His own. But it begins with you, learning to embody a Godly character yourself so that, in turn, you can recognize it in others. True Godliness will not be disguised by sheep in wolves' clothing. It is sincere, selfless, and steadfast, just as God intended.

To those who are seeking a pathway of understanding what this type of marriage looks like. To those who diligently seek self growth and insight that leads to a fulfillment that is difficult to explain and believe. To those who are committed to please God in and with their marriage, for God's glory.

This book is especially for those who have been faithful to the word of God in their lives and in marriage. A marriage after God's own heart.

Above all, this book is for our Father which is in Heaven. We thank God for this moment of insight. May this godly perception be a light to guide you—to guide us in recognizing His truth, preparing us for a marriage that mirrors His love—a love seeded in patience, kind, compassion, humility, and its truest form, for God's glory.

TABLE OF CONTENTS

ACKNOWLEDGEMENTS

This acknowledgement and honor and God's holiness for man's marriage goes out to Jesus Christ who has already shown us the way to a unified, loving marriage through His life, teachings, and ultimate sacrifice. In His selfless love, He demonstrated the grace, compassion, forgiveness, and commitment to devotion to the church that form the foundation of a marriage without division. His word calls us to commit. His word calls us to love one another as He has loved us, nurturing unity, humility, and selflessness in our relationships and marriages. Through Christ's example and the strength He offers, we are empowered to overcome division, forgive freely, and build marriages that reflect His love—serving as a testament to God's design for a harmonious, faithful union.

INTRODUCTION

The journey of life, filled with its myriad of experiences, beliefs, and challenges, has led me to a resounding conclusion: the union of two people joined together with a singular mission and vision is not a mere human connection but a profound, divine union. A union of choice—a choice to be one. A union under God's covenant. This union, designed by God, is one of selflessness, unity, and purpose. It is meant to be a living testimony—a reflection of His glory seen through the harmony, love, service and sacrifice shared between two as one. It is this conviction, born out of my own life's journey, that I wish to share with you in the pages of this book.

This book is a book for learning, surrendering, and understanding the purpose and power in a relationship forged to benefit God's glory. This book is essentially for everyone who believes in God's plan for marriage, who desires not a worldly successful marriage but a God-centered union. The beauty of such a union lies not just in the external expressions of love and commitment but in the deep, unwavering foundation built on faith, shared beliefs, surrender, and the understanding that life's greatest mission is to honor and glorify God in everything we do. This book aims to uncover the principles that make this possible, showing how two hearts (minds) can be one. When aligned as one in purpose and mission, this type of marriage can influence the world and create a legacy that speaks louder than words, and lasts longer than any materials left behind.

God's Marriage, at its core, is much more than just companionship. It is more than two people sharing a life, a home, or responsibilities. It is a spiritual covenant—a spiritual commitment that transcends the ordinary and steps into the sacred. It is a relationship that mirrors the unconditional love, grace, and unity that God shares with His creation. When two people come together with their minds and spirits rooted in the same beliefs and principles, their union becomes an embodiment of God's love. They become witnesses with their lives, not just to each other but to the world, of what it means to live in harmony, sacrifice, and deep mutual commitment.

What does it mean to be selfless in a godly marriage? How do two individuals, each with their own dreams, desires, and emotions, come together as one to pursue a higher calling? The answer lies in understanding God's love, the kind that pleases God, it's not about putting you first but placing the other person above yours. It's about understanding the nature of self and surrendering it to God's will. It is about self-restraint, compassion, and the joy found in lifting one another up, even when it's challenging and unwarranted. This book will guide us through what it takes to nurture such selflessness and how it looks—how it becomes second nature when the focus is on pleasing God first.

There is an extraordinary sense of peace and joy when a couple moves as one, not only in their actions but in their emotions, their minds, their will. When emotions are anchored in self-restraint and guided by wisdom, and when subconsciousness is fastened firmly to God's principles and led by the spirit, relationships flourish, life flourish. In such a relationship, conflicts are not sources of division but opportunities for growth, learning, and greater understanding. The two become a beacon of hope for others who observe them, showcasing how powerful unity can be when it is firmly rooted in God's principles and a constant focus on God's righteousness. When people see two individuals living as one harmonious unit, driven by shared beliefs and a deep love for God, they witness a testimony that words alone could never convey.

The inspiration for this book comes from my own life and experiences—times of joy, trials, growth, disappointments, and realization. Mainly from learning God's will for our lives for those who choose to marry and serve another. I realize relationships rooted in mutual understanding, love, trust, and an unyielding commitment to God's purposes brings out the best in both and reveals the God in them. Such a relationship can't compare to a partnership; it is a moving ministry. It becomes a source of strength, joy, and hope, not just for the couple but for everyone around them. It teaches that when you move as one, fueled by a mission greater than yourself, every interaction becomes a moment to glorify God and uplift others.

This book demonstrates this type of marriage is always a choice. This type of relationship is not established by feeling, it's a choice. This type of relationship is not sustained by chemistry, it's a choice. It is important to understand that this kind of marriage does not happen by chance; it requires deliberate effort, understanding, and, most importantly, a shared commitment to walk together in faith, discipline, obedience, and sacrifice. Simply put, it's a choice. This is a clear choice made by each other for each other, because of God. Each person must be willing to lay aside selfish desires, confront their weaknesses, become completely vulnerable and work through life's challenges with a spirit of humility, forgiveness and grace. Yes, this book is not for worldly marriages. This book will explore the tools and practices that can help us achieve this unity, from effective communication to shared spiritual practices and emotional management that build a strong, unshakeable foundation—forged in obedience to God's will.

The essence of such a union without division is about making each day count, seeing each interaction as an opportunity to live out the love and principles God has placed as a part of His will for us. Such a relationship like this places people above circumstances, above situations. It is about creating a legacy that touches the lives of others, leaving behind a powerful witness of God's goodness and grace in our life, in our relationships. This legacy is not built overnight but through consistent, loving, faith-filled thoughts and actions that speak of a life lived for more than personal gain. It is about what you impart to those you meet, the encouragement you provide, and the love you share that points others to a higher purpose. The power of such a relationship aligned with one mission and one vision can only be fully realized when both individuals commit to being one. This is a "one" in fusion, one will, one direction, one mission, one promise. The man must first understand this process in marriage. This starts with him assuring that he puts his wife's desires and cares within this mission in sacrifice. He must have the understanding on how to lead and cultivate his and her life, and she supports the process by his plans to do so. He puts her first and she submits to his lead, even when it is not easy, especially when it is not easy. This book will delve into what it means to act in ways that reflect God's will—practicing forgiveness, showing kindness, being patient, and choosing love every single day— God's Love. This book will guide you to understand that when two people become one in God's design, they create an unstoppable force, capable of impacting more than their family, community, it will also impact the heavens on earth.

I wrote this book with a full heart, knowing that the lessons and examples within it come from real hope and profound reflections, and godly intentions. My hope is that, as you read, you will find inspiration, encouragement, understanding, and practical guidance to strengthen your relationship; and for those single to prepare themselves for the one that may come into their lives. May your journey be one that shines as a testament to what God's love can do when two people commit to walking it out together, as one, for God sake.

I invite you to explore the pages ahead with an open heart and a desire to draw closer to God before you grow closer to one another. Especially if you are not married, this book is for you; a time to prepare. This book is not just about understanding relationships; it is about discovering the divine purpose behind them. Also, how they reflect God's love, and how they are a powerful force for His glory. May your relationship be one story of two people, united in mission and vision, moving as one, and leaving behind a legacy that speaks of God's goodness in your lives for generations to come.

CHAPTER 1
WHY A UNION
WITHOUT DIVISION

A Relationship for God – A Union Without Division

A union without division is for those seeking a relationship with God at the center. This type of relationship becomes an offering to God. A union chosen to honor God with their lives as a living sacrifice in everyday faithfulness and intentional decision to live in a way that reflects our love for God. A union without division is about faithfulness and obedience to be transformed by the renewing of your mind then you will be able to test and approve what God's will is for your marriage. This type of union is intentional. This type of marriage is to discover God's will for one another that their relationship is good, pleasing and perfect in God's will.

Why A Union Without Division:

Unfortunately, many of today's marriages are "all about me", my and mine. Especially in highly individualistic societies, people are increasingly influenced by self-gratification and social status. Marriage today is often seen as a vehicle for personal happiness, emotional support, or sexual fulfillment—rather than a covenant of mutual sacrifice, servitude, growth, and commitment. When those emotional, financial or physical needs aren't met, people many times feel justified in leaving or sabotaging the marriage, believing its purpose is primarily to satisfy them.

For some, marriage becomes a lifestyle upgrade or a societal checkbox—something to "complete" an image of success. The wedding, partner's appearance, social media image, and power couple optics often matter more than the substance of the person or the substance of the relationship. It's less about "us" as a unit and more about "how we look" as a couple. Many marriages today reflect a "what do I get?" approach—whether it's financial security, companionship, sexual satisfaction or social mobility. This creates a contract-like dynamic rather than a relational one, where love and commitment becomes conditional and disposable.

Sometimes many of us see the illusion of endless options from dating apps and social media when entering a marriage, some enter marriage with one foot out the door, fearing they're settling or could do better. Gratification becomes fleeting, and long-term commitment loses its value. The media often glorifies romance, luxury weddings, and "power couples" while downplaying the daily commitment and challenges, forgiveness, and humility marriage requires. This can skew expectations and foster a desire for instant gratification.

This book is to establish how to be a union without division. It's not "your money" or "my money"; it's our money. It's not "your things" or "my things"; it's our things. It's not "your way" or "my way"; it's our way. When two people live with this understanding, they no longer see themselves as competing individuals but as one team with a single mission, a single vision, working together for each other's benefit. With this mindset it embodies the relationship being each one is just parts of the body separately, but together they form the body. The relationship becomes a refuge, a sanctuary from life's challenges, where both individuals know they are supported, respected, and valued—not for what they do, but for who they are.

This way of living yields profound togetherness because it eliminates the barriers that often arise from selfish ambitions. It shifts the focus away from personal desires toward mutual well-being. In this relationship, it is always us against the world, never us against each other. Even if we started unevenly yoked, we became equally yoked. This is a decision. A decision made selflessly. This oneness allows for harmony—a deep sense of peace, a deep sense of joy that comes from knowing both partners are united in their purpose, values, and priorities; a submission to the other.

I invite those who believe in God's plan for marriage, if it truly requires compromise rather than sacrifice. The biblical model of marriage is not designed as a balance of rights or a system of fairness; it is grounded in *sacrifice* rather than *compromise*. Compromise implies a mutual concession where each partner gives up something to gain something in return. But God's design calls for something deeper—*sacrificial love.*

Ephesians 5:25 calls husbands to "love your wives, just as Christ loved the church and gave himself up for her." This is not a call to negotiate terms; it is a call to *selfless sacrifice.* Similarly, wives are called to submit "as to the Lord" (Ephesians 5:22), not because of the husband's merit but out of reverence for God. The goal is not equality in the sense of "you give a little, I give a little, or what do you bring to the table" but an *overflow of grace* that mirrors Christ's love for us.

Marriage is a sacred covenant where both partners are invited to embody *forgiveness, kindness, compassion,* and *patience* (Colossians 3:12-14). These virtues promote acceptance, not based on what the other person has earned or deserves, but because love—*agape love*—compels it. Acceptance in marriage isn't a compromise on standards; it's a surrender to God's transformative work, choosing to love as Christ loves us.

This book offers another outlook other than compromise and self interest. Instead of seeking fairness or equality, godly marriage calls for a constant state of serving and radical *sacrifice*—putting aside personal preferences and embracing *selfless* love. It's not about negotiating a middle ground but about extending grace upon grace, upon grace, trusting that in doing so, both partners are sanctified and blessed. This divine model doesn't simply aim for a functional relationship but for a *holy* one that reflects Christ's unconditional love.

The world constantly pressures godly marriages to conform to the concept of today's worldly marriages. These worldly marriages require those to perform to the worldly culture and seek selfish desires, but I urge those who desire to please God to seek a union without division. This concept of a union without division goes against the grain to live differently by allowing God to renew our minds. This renewal of the mind is essential to living in true freedom in a culture that often defines successful marriages as materialist and social status. This book challenges us to see life through God's eyes. Think about it, what would our lives look like if we saw everything through God's eyes, our relationships would no longer depend on the other person for our joy, peace or happiness. No more limitations, no more expectations, no more frustrations. No more need to try to focus on positive thinking rather replacing worldly thinking with God's perspective allowing his Spirit to shape how we see ourselves, others and his purpose for our lives. A true transformation that begins with surrender. Surrendering our own agendas and allowing God's spirit to reshape our hearts and minds and our purpose, so we find ourselves walking in God's will, a life marked by God's purpose peace and alignment a union of one, no more you or me only us. A marriage with His desires — as a Living Sacrifice in our relationships with His design. Living a union in love with sincere hate, for what is evil or not of God, cling to what is good or what is of God, being devoted to one another in love, honoring one another above yourself. A union committed to serve the other that seeks the best for the other. This type of union honors each other even when it's inconvenient, uncomfortable, and sometimes costly. It's a love that's rooted in forgiving and willing to mirror Christ's love for us.

A union without division is centered in God's grace, forgiveness, and mercy. Showing kindness through it all, always starting with mercy and humility ending with grace and forgiveness. A union living moment by moment relying on God's spirit to guide them in compassion and faithfulness letting go of pride embracing humility and recognizing that our strengths, talents and gifts are given to us to serve one another and others. In this union is a constant practice of dying to self daily. This union without division is to serve by seeing ourselves as part of a greater body of believers called to live sacrificially. It isn't just about our actions, it's about the posture of our hearts (minds), it's about recognizing that our lives are no longer our own, that we belong to God and our partner, and that God has a purpose for our union that goes beyond ourselves.

Have you ever considered that your marriage and your choices should be a living sacrifice that glorifies God's message in your lives and relationship as a testament to God? Have you considered your marriage has a purpose for God's ultimate plan? Have you considered living as a living sacrifice isn't about perfection it's about surrender. It's a daily decision to say God use me, God renew my mind, God help me to live in a way that honors you in this marriage. When we live this way we not only find fulfillment and purpose as believers we also become a light to those around us pointing others to God. Showing a God who loves, redeems and transforms us and demonstrates how blessed two who live like one are living a life of harmony. This is a union unified and an interconnected entity where each person has a role, a purpose and a gift for the other one to be edified, encouraged, and uplifted. Understanding this union each one has a different function so in Christ they are increased by belonging to one another in love.

God is calling those who chose to marry to step into marriage with faith (having complete trust in him) and to use whatever gift you have received to serve in your marriage first and then to serve with others as faithful stewards of God's grace. This calling for a union without division is meant for service not for personal gain. In a culture that often prizes individual achievement or recognition or personal gain, be reminded as a believer that our gifts are given not to elevate ourselves but to build up others and the Kingdom of God. Your gift should be prioritized to the one you have chosen to commit your life to and to the world. Imagine a union of that magnitude of deep unity and selflessness with humility and love. Imagine a sense of belonging not because of who you are but because who you belong to and who they are.

If we truly commit to this kind of love creating a space where each one feels worthy and accepted through God's purpose no matter their shortcomings. This call for a union without division isn't passive; it's an active choice to pursue harmony to be a peacemaker, a forgiver, and a giver of love in a world filled with division.

A love that sees even the smallest moments as opportunities to live out our faith to glorify God. Imagine what our communities and work places and families would look like if we took this concept of a union without division.

For those who still believe that a relationship like this can exist without deceit, selfishness, or self-centeredness. This book is for those who are not satisfied with the modern, transactional views of relationships, where personal gratification often overshadows faithfulness and sacrifice. Instead, this book offers a vision of love rooted in truth, humility, compassion, forgiveness, and faithfulness to God. A relationship not built on compromises and temporary agreements but one in which two people merge into a singular, God-honoring union. This union is not about convenience, negotiation, or partnership as society may define it, but about oneness—living, thinking, and growing as one entity.

A union without division is about a godly marriage in its truest sense—a merging of two hearts, minds, and lives into one. A relationship governed not by dual interests, but by a shared vision, purpose, and calling. Marriage is truly a choice, a choice willing to meet the call to love the other in sickness or in health, for richer or poorer, for better or worse, to cherish, until they are parted by death. This is not a call for the other to meet our needs. If we are careful to listen, these vows are for the other person and to the other person. When two people embrace this form of unity, they become more than just partners—they become one in spiritual flesh.

The Power of Mutual Submission:
A Relationship of Service, Not Compromise

Many people often view compromise as an essential component of maintaining harmony in relationships. The belief stems from the notion that compromise is a testament to mutual respect, validation, and the consideration of each other's viewpoints and personal values. At its surface, compromise seems to foster balance and strengthen bonds. When both partners bend to meet in the middle, it is perceived as a sign of shared commitment and teamwork, implying that each person values the other's happiness. This, in turn, creates a comforting illusion that their relationship is based on equality and fairness.

However, while compromise can be viewed as beneficial when done with clear boundaries and genuine respect, validating temporary solutions, it can also create a false sense of security and validation. The frequent act of compromising to preserve peace, self-gratification or gain temporary approval may lead to a subtle shift in the relationship dynamics. Instead of building an authentic, strong foundation, it can turn into a cycle where one or both partners continually compromise parts of themselves to avoid conflict or gain validation from the other. Over time, this can result in an unhealthy form of servitude, disguised under the guise of compromise.

The danger lies in repeated patterns where one person consistently makes concessions, leading to an unbalanced relationship. This can erode self-confidence and self-identity, as they may begin to suppress their true feelings, desires, and needs for the sake of the relationship. This form of constant self-sacrifice can feed the self-centered behaviors of the other partner, creating an environment where genuine mutual respect is lost. And one or the other is constantly feeling they must give up or give-in. While it may seem that compromise brings mutual respect, if one partner feels their the one mostly yielding, it sends a message that their needs and boundaries are less important.

In the long run, this approach only fosters a façade of harmony. Especially when either partner feels they're making continual sacrifices may experience feelings of resentment, emotional exhaustion, and a diminishing sense of self-worth. These underlying issues more than not will prevent the relationship from flourishing into a truly healthy and fulfilling bond, as one partner's constant yielding can inhibit authentic communication and personal growth. Many may believe that compromise reflects cooperation; submission may reflect imbalance or a loss of authority.

A union without division relationships are rooted in a healthy representation of their honest lifestyle, needs, and desires. When compatible and servitude align together. Also, in this type of union, their relationships are rooted in assertive communication and shared growth, where both partners' needs and values are recognized without one person's voice being consistently subdued. The key to a genuinely balanced relationship is not in blind compromise but in an ongoing desire to submit to the others needs and desires based on a compatible lifestyle, creating a space where both individuals can assert their needs and mutual desires, contributing to a thriving, reciprocal relationship.

Submission, submission, submission. Submission is a word often misunderstood and misapplied in relationships. Many assume it means one person losing their voice or individuality, their choices are under dictatorship, but true submission as intended by God is about willingly choosing to put the other person's needs above your own, not as a burden, but as an act of love, as an act of provision, or as an act of nurturing and care. When compatible—it's seamless and with chemistry—it's joyful. It is a relationship in which both partners seek to serve, honor, and care for each other without keeping score.

This is not a book about compromise, where both parties grudgingly meet halfway. This is not a book where both people get what they want and everyone gets their way. This is not a book about finding equality in a transactional sense, where everything must be divided evenly. Instead, it is about positioning oneself in accordance with God's design—where the man embraces his role as the leader and protector, and the woman flourishes in her role as the nurturer and supporter. These roles are not about dominance or inferiority but reflect the unique strengths God has given each individual to be together as one by God's standards.

This relationship is not centered on how you feel in the moment or what you believe you are entitled to. It is about what you have chosen to give. It is about how you surrender—relinquishing personal desires and agendas in favor of building something greater together. This is not a loss of self but a transformation of self—a deepening of one's purpose and identity within the context of believing in God's word. Submission! What!

I hope you are ready..

The Rewards of a God-Centered Union: Growth, Intimacy, and Stability

This is why a "A Union Without Division." This kind of union offers rewards far beyond what fleeting, self-serving relationships can provide. When two people submit to one another and live in accordance with God's design, they experience less stress and friction. More so they experience a joy unexplainable. Communication improves because both partners feel safe to express themselves and understand one another, knowing they will be heard and valued. Intimacy deepens as emotional walls are broken down, and both individuals feel seen and appreciated. Personal growth is inevitable, as each partner draws strength from the other's encouragement and support. This creates a sense of security and stability that cannot be easily shaken by life's challenges. When you choose to love someone not because of what they do for you but because you genuinely desire their well-being and you appreciate who they are, the relationship becomes a reflection of God's love. It is not just about being good to each other; it's also about being good for each other—encouraging, refining, and inspiring one another toward a godly relationship.

This book will guide couples through the process of building this kind of relationship and maintaining it for the long term, for a lifetime. It offers not just steps to get there but principles to sustain the ongoing journey of growth and unity. Relationships are not static; they require continual nurturing, adjustment, service, and care. Not work! The goal is not perfection in the absence of mistakes, but perfection with discipline, perfection with commitment, perfection with practice, perfection on purpose—where both individuals are aligned in their beliefs, values, and behaviors. Where work is not required. This type of godly union doesn't require work, only sacrifice. It becomes an alignment of unconscious movement.

Let's look at what can sometimes prevent a union without division to be sustainable.

Chapter 2
THE MAIN CAUSES IN THE BREAKDOWN OF MARRIAGES
Lack of Commitment, Dishonesty and Lack of Transparency

The way a marriage begins often determines how it will progress and ultimately finish. This doesn't mean failure, but it does matter how you start! Many people enter marriage with high hopes and aspirations, but the foundation upon which the relationship is built plays a pivotal role in whether those aspirations are fulfilled. While chemistry, communication, and shared interests are often seen as the cornerstones of a successful marriage, they are insufficient on their own to sustain a lifelong relationship. *Instead, the enduring qualities of commitment, honesty, transparency, awareness, and understanding form the godly foundation of a marriage capable of thriving through life's inevitable challenges. This is how!*

Commitment: The Main Point of Marriage — The Promise

The primary cause of the breakdown of many marriages is not a lack of love, chemistry, or communication, but a lack of true commitment. When couples enter marriage without fully understanding or embracing the depth of their commitment, they set themselves up for potential failure. This commitment is rooted in the covenant with God—it's not about convenience, feelings of love, or self-gratification. It is not about staying together only during the good times or when everything aligns perfectly or who does what and when. True commitment is tested during the hardships—when life presents challenges such as financial struggles, illness, self-gratification or emotional upheaval.

For many today, commitment is conditional—based on emotional fulfillment, mutual respect, financial conditions, and equality. When these fade or are no longer useful, so is the commitment. In many marriages, society increasingly values personal happiness, personal gain, and their autonomy, so commitment is often seen through the lens of "me, my or I" you know "I got to love myself first."

It's more common now for people to think "as long as it's good, I'm still in it." Rarely do we hear or see "no matter what, until death do us part." "No matter what!" And mean it, followed by its commitment.

A marriage built on a godly promise, one where both individuals make a deliberate choice to stand by each other under God's covenant, not for personal benefit, but primarily for the other person in selfless sacrifice. This kind of commitment requires a deep devotion with God and one another and involves honoring the other person by:

Giving: Choosing to prioritize their needs over your personal desires. Extremely generous with their time, energy, money and efforts to serve the other.

Forgiving: Letting go of the past hurts and choosing reconciliation over resentment. Letting go even when it isn't warranted. Not that person who says I don't forgive easily or it depends on the circumstances.

Trusting: Placing faith in their intentions and actions, even when doubts arise, even when they failed before. Then they go to God and place their trust in Him.

Submitting: Humbly yielding to each other's needs and well-being, fostering unity rather than dominance or selfishness.

Honesty: And the highest pillar in honoring the other person by being completely honest. The Pillar that lead to Trust

Honesty is the main component of stability of any successful relationship, and in marriage, it holds unparalleled importance. A marriage that does not start on a foundation of honesty is unlikely to sustain joy, health, unity or longevity. Honesty is more than simply telling the truth; it is about living in a way that reflects integrity, authenticity, and openness. It is about telling how one truly lives. In a marriage, honesty fosters:

Trust: When both partners consistently act in truthful ways, they build confidence in each other's words and actions. They say what the do and do what they say.

Security: Knowing that your partner is honest creates a sense of safety and stability within the relationship.

Clarity: Honesty opens the door to transparency that eliminates confusion and misunderstandings, allowing for clearer communication and connection.

However, honesty on its own is insufficient without its companion: transparency.

Transparency: The Gateway to Truth

While honesty involves telling the truth, transparency takes it a step further by ensuring that nothing is hidden. Transparency eliminates the gaps that can lead to doubt or suspicion. It allows both partners to see the complete picture of who the other person is—their desires, fears, struggles, and dreams.

Transparency in marriage creates an environment where:

Vulnerability is embraced: Both partners feel safe enough to share their innermost thoughts and feelings without fear of judgment. This strengthens their security in the relationship. Doubts are erased: When nothing is hidden, there is no room for secrets or deception, fostering deeper trust.

Authenticity thrives: Transparency allows both individuals to be fully themselves, strengthening the bond between them. The first step towards acceptance.

For transparency to truly flourish, it must be mutual. Both partners must be willing to shine a light on every area of their lives that touches their relationship, from their past experiences to their current struggles and future aspirations. This openness forms the foundation of a relationship where both individuals feel seen, heard, understood, and more so accepted. Be careful if one doesn't really want to hear the other's past. Some people believe you should only reveal what is necessary and what's important. And if it is hurtful and not necessary, be careful. Ask about what you are willing to accept and ask yourself if you are a forgiving person without judgement, especially in the beginning of a relationship, seek counseling if needed. This process takes an ongoing requirement of devotion and compassion.

The Synergy of Commitment, Honesty, and Transparency

When commitment, honesty, and transparency are present in a marriage, they create a synergy that prevents breakdowns and paves the way for a flourishing relationship. These qualities are not merely ideals to strive for—they are practical and part of the formula for a union without division, daily practices that shape the way both partners approach their union and tightens their bond. They foster four results:

1. **Resilience**: A committed marriage does not crumble under pressure but grows stronger through challenges. When honesty and transparency are part of this commitment, couples can address problems head-on, finding solutions together rather than letting issues fester.

2. **Intimacy**: Emotional, physical, and spiritual intimacy thrives in an environment of openness and trust. When your partner believes you are fully committed to them, intimacy and openness moves effortlessly. Honesty and transparency ensure that there are no barriers to genuine connection.

3. **Respect**: Commitment grounded in selflessness, honesty, and transparency fosters deep respect for one another. This respect forms the basis of a relationship where both partners feel valued, honored and liked.

4. **Love that Endures**: Love in marriage is not just an emotion but an action—a choice to remain devoted despite challenges. A choice to be patient in difficult times. A choice to be kind to your partner when they are not kind to you. A choice to forgive when it's not deserved. When couples build their marriage on the pillars of commitment, honesty, and transparency, their love is reinforced daily, making it stronger and more enduring. When these things are practiced regularly they invoke a desire for devotion.

Such scenery goes beyond the fleeting expectations of material success or external validation. Instead, it is about finding and cherishing a partner who shares your principles, beliefs, and values even when it's difficult. When two people are aligned in their core convictions, their commitment is not merely to each other but to directly bind with God with a shared vision of what marriage represents. This mutual understanding creates a solid foundation for a relationship—a union without division can weather any storm.

Transforming Commitment to Devotion

Creating devotion in a marriage is not a one-time act but a continuous, intentional journey that deepens love, appreciation, and connection—more and more over time. Here are some key steps to cultivate devotion in a godly marriage:

1. Prioritize God Together

Devotion begins with both spouses seeking God first (Matthew 6:33). Praying together, reading Scripture, studying together and worshiping as a couple nurture spiritual unity. This shared pursuit helps each partner draw closer to God, which naturally draws them closer to each other.

2. Practice Selfless Love

Devotion grows when each spouse puts the other's needs above their own (Philippians 2:3-4). This means listening without interrupting, serving without expecting anything in return, not putting demands on one another, and respecting each other even when it's hard. Selflessness builds trust, breaks down barriers, inspires mutual giving, and offers a sense of safety, fostering deep commitment.

3. Communicate Regularly and Honestly

Open, honest communication nurtures connection. Also, having a clear understanding of your partner and their experiences. Share your thoughts, dreams, and struggles, and encourage your spouse to do the same. Avoid criticism and practice gentle, affirming speech (Ephesians 4:29). Devotion grows stronger when both feel heard and valued. Communicating regularly doesn't mean talking for hours and hours every day just to talk. Respect one another's time, space, and solitude to reflect and grow as well.

4. Create Shared Rituals

Creating simple habits like praying together before bed, sharing a morning coffee or devotional studying, or planning a weekly "date night" reinforce your commitment and reinforce your devotion. These rituals become anchors in the relationship, expressing your dedication to one another. Remember there is group time and there's a couple times, have balance.

5. Forgive and Extend Grace

Regularly practicing forgiveness and extending grace. Conflict is inevitable, rather it's with you guys or against you guys, but consistent devotion thrives when forgiveness is freely given (Colossians 3:13). Let go of grudges, avoid keeping score, and choose to move forward in love. Grace keeps bitterness from taking root and reflects God's love. The key is to let go, let go and remember to let go.

6. Show Appreciation and Affection

My favorite. Express gratitude for your spouse's qualities, contributions and their presence. Physical touch, kind words, and acts of service strengthen the emotional bond. These daily acts of love communicate devotion more powerfully than words.Don't forget to say I appreciate you and say it often. Do this a lot! And don't stop even when moments and situations don't warrant it.

Preventing Breakdown and Cultivating a Flourishing Relationship

Preventing the breakdown of a relationship requires ongoing attention, intentional habits, and emotional maturity. Here's some way how:

1. Prioritize Open Communication

Seek to understand yourself first and then your partner. This means become aware of how you communicate and how they communicate. Speak honestly about feelings, needs, and concerns, don't wait; unless you are angry. Listen to understand, not just to respond. Address issues early—don't let resentment build. Men do this for women, listen more, as much as you can and be patient.

2. Commit to Emotional Safety

Avoid blame, criticism, or contempt. Show empathy and validate your partner's emotions and validate their concerns. Create a safe space where both can be vulnerable. Even if you both agree to a certain place in the home where you both agree to be completely respectful and patient when communicating difficult issues. Women do this for men, never disclose to others what that man has shared with you in confidence to others, no matter how hurt you are.

3. Invest in Quality Time

Regularly connect beyond routines—again, date nights, shared activities, deep conversations. Be fully present, even in small moments, especially in small moments. Be sincerely concerned about the other person's situations outside of martial issues.

4. Again, Practice Forgiveness and Grace

Accept that both partners will make mistakes. Forgive quickly and seek resolution instead of revenge. Also, quickly forgive others close to you both so those emotional ties won't filter into your relationship, affecting your relationship.

5. Nurture Physical Intimacy, Emotional Intimacy, and Spiritual Intimacy as the Center

On this one let's expand.

Be affectionate—touch, compliments, meaningful gestures. Talk about desires, principles, and needs openly. Pray for one another openly, daily and with one another daily.

Men

As a man one must be emotionally grounded and spiritually rooted. He must lead with gentleness, never harsh or dismissive with his partner. Be gentle even in truth. When your partner is overwhelmed or discouraged, listen without rushing to fix things. He offers a calm presence, a soft shoulder, he offers a safe place for her to emote, praying with her and speaking words of life and encouragement. Spiritually, he covers their home in prayer, reads the Word and studies regularly to be the example. He practices not letting any stress, drama or attacks from her to be personal. He never expects her to initiate forgiveness or patience for he knows this is his responsibility over her. He provides grace and patience when she doesn't deserve it. His focus is on humility and consistency not trying to dominate or be right, rather invite peace and love in her life through his ways. He knows he is limited in himself as he champions her, always pointing her back to Christ. He leads with God's principles.

Women

As a woman one must be aware and understanding of the nature of a man. She must submit to his presence, meaning she must not try to control or overpower him in any way, at any time for any reason. When her partner is not performing at his best or not showing up as he should, she doesn't use her words to disrespect him. She offers grace, she offers prayer, she encourages him even when he doesn't see it in himself or he has no confidence in himself. She inspires him to be better by demonstrating her commitment to him, not because of his potential or what he offers, but because of the god in him, she reassures him she is committed to him especially when his spirits are low, his performance is weak, and his contributions are little. She discerns his emotional needs even when he's quiet. When he struggles, she doesn't nag or push—she prays, listens, and speaks truth with love and compassion. She regularly reminds him of his value in God's eyes, his value to her and affirms his leadership in her life as a need in respectful ways. She practices giving him nourishment with her acts of caring for him daily. She consistently builds a relationship with God to develop a nature of empathy, compassion and submission. She develops a habit of prayer making a safe place for her partner to be vulnerable. She leads with God's principles not hers or the worlds.

Together they create a home where emotional and physical needs are met with awareness and understanding that allows grace and acceptance to always be present. They also create spiritual needs to connect them beyond the physical with intentional acts of purpose. And they don't forget to laugh together, share moments of interest together, and regularly engage in playful banter.

To nurture a physical connection along with practicing emotional intimacy and building a spiritual bond are at the center of a devotional godly marriage.

6. Know and Respect Boundaries

Not in a worldly way. Know each other's limits and triggers that they are currently working on. Be intentional and work with helping them. Balance togetherness with healthy independence. Allow grace in each interaction. Lead with empathy and compassion. Always be practicing on doing away with having triggers. Godly marriages have no triggers.

7. Keep Growing The Relationship

Encourage each other's personal development. Encourage each other's spiritual growth. We are never done. Share dreams, set goals, and evolve as a team. More importantly spend lots of intentional quality time and solitude with meditation and in prayer.

8. Seek Help When Needed

Don't wait until things are falling apart, seek self help through God's word and reflect, reflect and reflect. Awareness. If necessary seek counseling or mentorship. First seek God's word for direction and understanding before seeking a wise third party for complex issues.

Cultivating a flourishing relationship starts with the man. He needs to understand both his nature and her nature and is ready to lead. This is not about control, it is about leadership, servitude, and sacrifice. This is about his leadership through his love, security, and understanding. A man cultivates a woman by creating the right emotional, spiritual, and relationship environment for her to thrive. Here's how:

1. Create Emotional Safety
Be consistent, honest, and dependable. Keep your word! Avoid unpredictable anger, criticism, or silence. Let her feel safe to express her full self without fear of rejection or judgment. This also means a lot of listening.

2. Listen Deeply and Attentively
Don't rush to fix her emotions—hear her heart. What does that mean? Ask questions that invite her to share more of why. Validate her feelings, even if you don't fully understand them.

3. Lead with Care and Stability, Not Control
Offer direction and purpose, but invite her perspective. Make decisions that reflect care for both of you. Build trust by being re-

sponsible with your words, actions, and time. Speak carefully and mean what you say.

4. Speak Life into Her

Affirm her identity, beauty, gifts, and growth. Notice the small things she does and speak gratitude often. Your words shape how she sees herself and you.

5. Encourage Her Passions and Purpose

Support her dreams, goals, and interests. Include her dreams and interests into yours, don't treat them separately. Don't compete with her strength—celebrate it. Help her believe she can rise without losing you.

6. Maintain Your Own Emotional Balance

A grounded man brings peace to a relationship. Handle your emotions maturely, even if she doesn't—don't make her your emotional regulator. Be vulnerable first. Be willing to let your feelings be hurt to save hers.

7. Protect Her Peace

Shield her from unnecessary stress or emotional chaos. You don't need to tell her everything if it's not necessary, especially if it will hurt her for no reason. Discern when to step in and when to simply stand with her. Set boundaries with others that honor your union. Protect her from the outsiders. When a woman feels emotionally safe, seen, and supported, she naturally blossoms offering back love, loyalty, and wisdom; this is masculine stewardship.

The presence of commitment, honesty, and transparency in a marriage does more than just prevent breakdowns; it sets the stage for a relationship that thrives, that represents, that performs. Marriages that lack these qualities often find themselves vulnerable to misunderstandings, resentment, outside influences, and eventual separation. By contrast, marriages that embrace these principles create an environment where love, honor, and respect flourish. This kind of marriage is not focused on individual satisfaction or material gain. Instead, it is rooted in the mutual decision to build a life together that is meaningful and fulfilling.

This is a marriage where both partners:

Choose unity over division: They work together as a one unit, valuing the relationship above personal gain, pride or ego.

Prioritize growth: They invest in each other's well-being, supporting personal and a shared mission.

Live with integrity: They consistently align their actions with their principles, ensuring that their relationship remains a source of joy and stability.

A marriage like this begins with a life commitment built on selflessness, a foundation of honesty, and a commitment of transparency is one that has the best chance of thriving, lasting, and loving, and representing God's will. While chemistry, communication, and shared interests may bring people together, they cannot sustain a lifelong union alone. True success in marriage comes from the daily choice to prioritize these deeper qualities and serve the other person.

Commitment ensures that both partners remain steadfast through life's ups and downs. Honesty builds a foundation of trust and security. Transparency fosters openness and understanding. Together, these qualities create a marriage that is resilient, intimate, and enduring—a marriage that not only survives but flourishes. When couples embrace these principles from the start, they set themselves on a path toward a relationship that honors their values, strengthens their bond, and creates a legacy of love and partnership.

As I mentioned, usually the way a marriage begins often determines how it will progress and ultimately finish. The other main cause in the breakdown of marriage, you guessed it, infidelity. When aspirations dissipate and chemistry is gone, and our communication in the relationship rarely shows up—thoughts of infidelity are always lurking around the corner.

CHAPTER 3
THE OTHER CAUSE IS INFIDELITY

You Are Not Yours

Many breakdowns of many marriages can often be attributed to infidelity, a betrayal that undermines trust and fractures the bond between spouses. Infidelity, however, is rarely the root cause; it is often a symptom of deeper issues such as lack of communication, lack of commitment, dishonesty, emotional disconnection, or unmet needs. When a marriage is forged in commitment and devotion, coupled with a profound understanding of its purpose, the likelihood of infidelity becomes almost non-existent. Such a union is characterized by mutual understanding, self-awareness, and a commitment that transcends individual desires, grounding the relationship in principles not feelings that create a sanctuary of love and trust. This leads to the understanding that you are not yours.

A marriage built on love and understanding begins with a shared awareness of its purpose. A godly marriage is more than feelings and gratification, and more than a social or legal contract; it is a covenant. It is a covenant rooted in the desire to support, uplift, share, and grow alongside another person. When both partners embrace this vision, they approach the relationship with intentionality, ensuring that their actions, decisions, and interactions align with their shared values. This understanding establishes a foundation where each individual not only commits to their partner but also recognizes their responsibilities within the relationship and a belonging to the other is present. You are not yours in a godly marriage.

Central to these responsibilities is the commitment to facilitate each other's emotional and physical needs. We cannot always meet the other person's needs but we can always be willing to facilitate and have compassion for the other person. A marriage rooted in love and understanding acknowledges the importance of fulfilling sexual desires as an expression of intimacy and trust. In such relationships, both partners view this aspect of their union not as an obligation but as a joyful act of giving. They prioritize open communication about their needs and desires, fostering a dynamic of mutual respect and care. By consistently nurturing this dimension of their relationship, they create an environment where both individuals feel valued, desired, and secure.

Moreover, a marriage grounded in commitment and understanding promotes high and consistent self-esteem for both partners. This is because each individual recognizes that their worth is not derived from their spouse but from their core principles, beliefs, and relationship with their Creator. This self-awareness allows them to engage in the marriage from a place of wholeness, rather than seeking validation or fulfillment solely from their partner. They understand that while their spouse can complement their journey, true self-worth comes from living in alignment with God revealing their values and purpose.

This sense of self-worth also ensures that destructive behaviors such as anger, neglect, or narcissism find no foothold in this type of relationship. In a marriage forged in God's love, both partners actively work to support each other's emotional and spiritual well-being. They approach challenges with patience and empathy rather than resorting to blame or manipulation. By prioritizing open dialogue and mutual respect, they create a safe space where vulnerabilities can be shared without fear. This eliminates the conditions that often lead to resentment, withdrawal, or toxic patterns.

Daily emotional connection is a hallmark of such a marriage. Both partners understand that this type of companionship is not static but an ongoing practice. They invest time and energy in nurturing their bond through meaningful conversations, shared experiences, and acts of kindness. This consistent effort reinforces their commitment and keeps their relationship vibrant and fulfilling. Their dedication to emotional intimacy ensures that they remain attuned to each other's needs, preventing the drift that can make a relationship vulnerable to external temptations.

Ultimately, the most powerful safeguard against infidelity in a marriage forged in love and understanding is the couple's shared commitment to something greater than themselves, God. They view their union not merely as a relationship but as a divine calling, A ministry. This perspective transforms their relationship into a sacred bond, one that demands surrender, sacrifice, and unwavering devotion. Their decision to give themselves fully to one another—physically, emotionally, and spiritually—is not contingent on circumstances but is rooted in an unshakable resolve to honor their covenant.

This type of surrender is profound, as it goes beyond transactional love. It reflects a willingness to give and receive without conditions, even in moments of imperfection or challenge. This commitment transcends physical attraction, fleeting emotions, or external pressures. Instead, it is anchored in the understanding that their marriage is a reflection of their values and their faith. By surrendering to each other "despite everything," they create a union where love is steadfast, trust is unbreakable, and infidelity is inconceivable.

In conclusion, a marriage forged in God's love and understanding is a relationship defined by mutual surrender, shared purpose, and unwavering commitment. It thrives on emotional connection, spiritual commitment, self-awareness, and the recognition that both individuals are part of something far greater than themselves—a marriage. This kind of marriage leaves no room for infidelity because its foundation is built on principles not chemistry, principles that prioritize giving, trust, forgiving, and faith— based on a singular understanding.

Chapter 4
A Relationship Forged in Love, Not Circumstance or Lust

Sacrifice, Service, and Selflessness

God's love is not built on convenience, fleeting attraction, or personal gain. It is not based on situations or circumstances but on a deliberate choice to love and serve another person. This is the kind of love that sustains a marriage through both joy and hardship. It is a love that seeks to give rather than take, to bless rather than demand, and to uplift rather than criticize. It is a love rooted in God's example—a love that sacrifices, forgives, and endures—a union without division.

This book is for those who long to experience the fullness of that kind of love—a love not swayed by feelings or circumstances but anchored in faith, commitment, devotion and service. It is for those who desire to live out the true meaning of a godly marriage: two people becoming one, united in mind, spirit, and purpose. One flesh.

This relationship is not about meeting each other halfway or negotiating terms. It is about fully embracing one another—flaws and all—and choosing to grow together through it all, not because of it all. It is about living as one entity, perfectly aligned not because you are identical, but because you fit each other like a hand that fits the glove. A complement of principles, beliefs, and long-term behaviors.

Living in Your God-Given Roles: Masculinity and Femininity in Harmony

A union without division emphasizes the importance of embracing the unique attributes of masculinity and femininity in its fullness. In a world that often blurs these distinctions, if we recognize the beauty of God's design—how the strengths of one partner enhance and bless the other, creating a harmonious balance—what a treasure. In a marriage men are called to lead, protect, and provide, while women are called to nurture, support, and inspire. When these roles are understood and embraced, the relationship flourishes.

It is not about finding someone to meet your desires or conforming to societal norms, but about celebrating the unique ways in which men and women reflect God's image as one body—in biology, emotionally, psychologically, and physically.

The Perfect Union: Not Without Flaws, But Perfect in Purpose

A perfect marriage is not one without mistakes, disagreements, or challenges. It is not about achieving an ideal, flawless state. Instead, perfection in a marriage lies in its unity—in the way two people choose to live, love, and grow together as God's design, despite their imperfections or their differences. It is perfect in its intention, perfect in its faithfulness, and perfect in its pursuit of a shared purpose. Perfect in its union.

Let's explore how couples can cultivate this kind of relationship, how they can overcome obstacles, and how they can continue to grow in love and faith throughout their journey together. This book is not just a guide to starting a strong relationship; it is a representation for sustaining and deepening that relationship over a lifetime.

A union without division is for those who want more than just happy moments in a relationship—they want a relationship that honors God, reflects His love, and brings out the best in both partners, and forgives the worst in both partners for God's sake. It is a call to live not by the world's standards but by God's design. A call to love by God's standards, embracing the power and beauty of becoming one—back to the basics.

This union begins with understanding the differences and its impact in masculine and feminine energy. Masculine energy is usually active in its actions and assertive in its motive to provide and protect. Feminine energy is usually facilitated with communication and compassion driven to desire to comfort and invite with harmony and cooperation. When these energies are connected they eliminate competition, control, pressure and chaos. They unite in empathy, togetherness, and in creation. It's important to understand God's design and His plan has a divine purpose and these are not to be looked at as barriers but strengths each one has to enrich the other.

Loving one another in their own attributes as masculine and feminine is about appreciating and embracing God's plan for humanity rooted not in our own understanding. This doesn't diminish the other, it strengthens both when they both choose to surrender to a union without division.

When Solidity Meets Warmth

A Godly relationship is shaped by the divine balance of masculine and feminine energy. Not competition. Not Domination. Not sameness. But in submission to complement the other. Two unique forces that were never designed to mirror each other, or to compete with each other, but only to aid each other.

When a man embraces his God-given masculine nature and a woman fully steps into her feminine essence, something powerful happens:

This harmony creates a union where each partner receives the benefit of the other's natural design, and together they form a relationship marked by peace, connection, respect, and unity.

They stop fighting for roles,
and they begin flowing in harmony.

This harmony creates a union where each partner receives the benefit of the other's natural design, and together they form a relationship marked by peace, connection, respect, and unity.

This is the beauty of *A Union Without Division*: two people becoming one through the strengths that God handcrafted within them.

This harmony creates a union where each partner receives the benefit of the other's natural design, and together they form a relationship marked by peace, connection, respect, and unity.

1. The Blessings a Woman Receives When a Man Walks in Healthy Masculinity

A man grounded in masculine strength brings more than presence—he brings protection, stability, direction, and emotional security. His energy sets the foundation of the relationship, giving his woman room to relax, breathe, and blossom.

He Creates Emotional and Physical Safety

Safety and trust is the bedrock of love for a woman. When a man embodies protector energy:

A woman feels safe enough to trust. She can soften without fear. Her heart can open without hesitation. His consistency and reliability become a shield around her emotional world. He becomes her anchor of stability. Masculine energy is steady, dependable, and rooted. A place to rest emotionally and build confidence in the relationship's future. This creates ease and freedom in her feminity. Freedom from carrying the relationship alone. When done right his structure becomes her sanctuary.

He Provides Direction and Vision

Masculinity brings clarity and leadership. A woman benefits from:

A man who moves with purpose and understanding. A man who doesn't drift, but decides how and when to move forward giving her the benefit of not worrying. A partner who leads through actions, not intentions gives a strong sense of peace of where they are heading. His direction gives their union momentum and meaning. He cultivates growth because masculine energy builds. It improves, it protects, and it sustains.

A woman thrives under:

A man who invests in himself and the relationship. Masculine energy invokes a man who takes responsibility for its development. A man who seeks progress, not perfection. His cultivation strengthens their love over time and inspires her feminine to flourish. A masculine man naturally draws out a woman's warmth, softness, receptivity, and joy. His strength makes her feel cherished, valued, and chosen. In this harmony, both partners rise.

2. The Blessings a Man Receives When a Woman Walks in Healthy Femininity

Where masculine energy stabilizes, feminine energy increases and provides softens, warms, and enriches their environment. A woman in her feminine nature brings a positive emotional life, connection, and healing into the relationship. She becomes the heart to his structure, the warmth to his strength, the nurturing presence to his leadership.

She is comfortable creating emotional connections. Feminine energy invites closeness, communication, and depth.

A man benefits from:

A connection that softens his stress. A feminine woman turns a house into a home and a relationship into a sanctuary. She offers:

Emotional and physical nurturing and an inviting energy, she becomes magnetic. She brings a soothing presence and softness that balances his strength. Her warmth relaxes him in ways the world cannot. She inspires him to lead and provide through submission. True femininity calls greatness out of a man. It invites his protection, his ambition, his devotion and his desires to rise higher. A man thrives with a woman who believes in him and sees his heart and true intentions.

3. The Harmony of Two Energies Working Together

When both partners embrace their natural strengths, the relationship transforms. There is no competition — only cooperation. There are no struggles for power or control — only shared purpose. There is no division — only unity within the union shaped by design. Together he protects and provides; she nurtures and supports. He leads and cultivates; she embraces and connects.

This is the blueprint of a union without division — not because they are the same, but because they bring their differences to bring out the best of who they are for the good of the relationship.

4. When Masculinity and Femininity Unite, Love Becomes Effortless

There is a natural rhythm that emerges when healthy masculine and feminine energies join. Attraction deepens, respect increases, trust flows, passion intensifies, peace settles in the home and partnership becomes a relationship again.

In this harmony, marriage becomes more than a transactional commitment — it becomes a calling, a ministry and a reflection of God's design.

This is the beauty of a marriage where both partners embrace who they were meant to be. The essence of *A Union Without Division* brings us back to the basics.

Chapter 5
Back to the Basics
The Purpose of Marriage
The Marriage God Intended

The foundation of a godly marriage between a man and a woman who chooses to care for one another as partners is built on certain essential, and timeless values. At its core, this connection is about genuine servitude, where each partner values the other for who they truly are as a person, not for what they can get or what they do. This connection is rooted in mutual desire, spiritual beliefs, respect, shared values, and deep spiritual support, creating a bond that fosters trust and intimacy.

This connection is about genuine desire for shared values of wanting to share their lives. A connection where decisions like having children, both desire to procreate or not because of what they value and why. This is not a compromise, these choices must be what they both want. When these types of decisions are embraced within this relationship, it is seen not only as a biological function but as a profound act of unity and legacy. It becomes a natural extension of their commitment, with both partners nurturing life together and raising a family in a shared journey of love and responsibility.

Additionally, when their union is anchored in faith and God's grace, it provides a spiritual foundation that enriches their relationship. This spiritual grounding emphasizes the importance of commitment and sanctity, steering them away from a life of selfishness, instead promoting compassion and respect. By living in accordance with these core beliefs, the relationship transcends mere companionship and becomes a sacred view of partners where love, purpose, and faith intertwine, creating a resilient and enduring union.

Marriage, as God intended, is a beautiful union of two souls who come together not just to meet each other's needs, but to glorify God through their relationship through their needs. It is a covenant that reflects God's love for His people, with the husband and wife serving distinct yet complementary roles. In such a marriage, both partners are committed to growing in love, patience, and wisdom, working together to create a life rooted in God's will.

A husband rooted in God's will understands that his role as the leader of the family is not about control but about stewardship. He models Christ's love by leading with humility, patience, and kindness. His leadership is not a burden but a responsibility he embraces with joy, knowing he is accountable to God for the responsibility and well-being of his family. He is financially disciplined, ensuring that his household is provided for and protected from unnecessary hardships. Emotionally intelligent, he responds with empathy when his family faces difficulties, offering guidance and support rather than harsh correction or reacting out of emotions.

This man sees his role as a cultivator, bringing out the best in his wife and children by continually learning, growing, and sharing in understanding. He establishes structure and order within the household, not to dominate but to ensure peace and harmony. His authority is rooted in God's principles, and he models integrity by living a life that is consistent both in public and private. His words are deliberate, his promises are kept, and his silence is wise. He washes his wife with the Word of God, reassuring her of his love and commitment to God and her, not through mere words, but through daily actions of care, concern, and honor.

The wife, likewise, is rooted in God's will and fully aware of her accountability to both God and her husband. She understands that her submission to her husband is not a loss of power but a path to peace and joy. She understands her submission does not mean inferiority; it means strength and willingly aligning her vision with her husband's to avoid division. She walks alongside her husband, assisting him and directing him toward righteousness when needed, not as a critic but as a helper. She gives generously of her time and resources to him and others, enriching everything she touches.

She knows that her ultimate wholeness comes not from her husband but from God, and she surrenders herself fully to Him. Her life is marked by selflessness and kindness, as she seeks the good of her family and others over her own pleasures. Her home becomes a sanctuary—a warm, inviting space where her husband can find rest and renewal. She understands that her beauty lies not just in her appearance but in her manners, warmth, and care. Her femininity is expressed in how she nurtures, encourages, and supports her husband and children, ensuring that love and peace reign in their home. This type of woman understands her biggest strength lies in her self-restraint and ability to surrender.

In this marriage, this couple submits to one another out of reverence for God. The husband leads not for his own benefit but for the glory of God, ensuring that his wife feels cherished and secure. He communicates with empathy, always striving to understand her needs and calm her fears. He is eager to listen, to nurture her emotional well-being, and to cultivate her growth. His love is not contingent on perfection but rooted in grace, and he is quick to forgive and slow to anger. Even when they are apart, his actions reflect his commitment to her, as he lives with integrity and honor. He leads with honesty.

The wife, in turn, delights in her role as a source of comfort and care for her husband. She values his leadership and demonstrates appreciation for his presence and knowledge in her life. She trusts him completely even when she doesn't agree, allowing herself to lean into his care without the need to control or dictate. This wife releases all her control over her husband. Yes. She understands their motivations differ and respects his role even when she doesn't understand or agree in the midst of challenges. Her words are gentle, her heart is open, and her actions reflect a deep desire to bring joy and peace to God and their marriage.

This marriage is a union of two selfless souls fused together, each focused not on what they can receive but on what they can give. The husband considers his wife's well-being in every decision, while the wife seeks the best for her husband at all times. It is a relationship where two become one, united not just in body but in spirit and purpose. In this oneness, they reflect the love of Christ for His Church—a love that is patient, kind, forgiving, and enduring.

This kind of marriage is not free from challenges, but the couple faces them together, rooted in their shared faith and trust in God. Believing that everything is not going to go their way but God's way. They forgive easily, love deeply, and grow continuously, knowing that their union is a reflection of God's divine plan. Their home becomes a beacon of hope and love, a place where God's presence is felt and His principles are lived out daily. This is the marriage God intended—one of harmony, mutual understanding, and unwavering commitment to God and serving each other, always striving to glorify Him in all things.

Chapter 6
Awareness And Under-standing

Awareness, Understanding and Prayer:
The Glue to God's Marriage

Ultimately, awareness and understanding form the foundation of a strong person, and a healthy marriage. They allow couples to navigate the complexities of trust, communication, and emotional connection with greater ease. When couples are aware of their own emotions and behaviors, as well as the needs and perspectives of each other, they can build a relationship based on mutual respect, empathy, and love

Understanding the foundation of a healthy relationship is essential for fostering lasting, meaningful connections. Healthy relationships are built on mutual respect, trust, empathy, and a commitment to understanding and serving each other's needs. Awareness of these elements helps individuals navigate challenges and grow together rather than apart.

However, when relationships are viewed through the lens of a partnership, problems can arise. The concept of partnership originated in the business world, emphasizing shared responsibilities, equal stakes, and joint outcomes. This approach values goal accomplishment over nurturing emotional bonds, which can be detrimental when applied to personal relationships. Couples who focus on balancing responsibilities or benefits can fall into a transactional mindset, assessing whether each partner is contributing equally. This mindset may foster competition or resentment, as the relationship becomes more about measuring contributions and fairness than genuine care and support.

Healthy relationships, in contrast, center on serving and uplifting each other selflessly. They prioritize the emotional and spiritual growth of both partners, fostering a sense of unity and love that cannot be reduced to the rigid give-and-take of business-style partnerships. Embracing this difference shifts relationships from strategic conditioned cooperation to heartfelt connection, ensuring they thrive on compassion, not calculations.

Today's marriage is often described as a partnership built on trust and communication, and while these are crucial pillars, they are not the foundation upon which a healthy, enduring God relationship is built. The real essence of a successful God marriage lies in awareness, understanding and prayer—with a commitment to the marriage. Without these, trust can falter, communication can become ineffective, and partners can feel misunderstood, regardless of how frequently they speak to each other or exchange promises. Awareness and understanding allow couples to go beyond surface-level interactions and foster deep emotional connections, and with consistent prayer cements spiritual bonds. This combination builds longevity and a clear understanding and ultimately creates a space where love can grow, evolve, and thrive through the everyday challenges of life.

Again, many believe that trust and communication are the bedrock of any relationship. While both are essential parts to the pillars of relationships, they are outcomes of something deeper: understanding the other person and having the self-awareness to navigate your own emotions and behaviors in the midst of disagreements, chaos, and confusion is key to a healthy trusting and effective communication. Even with clear communication and attempts to build trust, relationships can falter if neither partner understands the underlying motivations, fears, shames, and vulnerabilities that drive their behavior. Communication without understanding may lead to more frustration than resolution, and trust cannot be fully cultivated without an environment of emotional safety and empathy.

Trust is directly related to honesty, transparency, and loyalty. Trust also invites the desires to be vulnerable. This awareness and understanding is pivotal. In order for trust to grow and flourish one must be vulnerable and aware of their emotional stability. Trust is not merely about avoiding betrayal or dishonesty; it is about creating an emotional space where both partners feel free to express their insecurities, fears, and flaws without judgment. This level of trust requires a profound understanding of one another's needs, desires, shame, and fears. Without awareness of how trust is built through emotional vulnerability, couples may unconsciously engage in behaviors that create emotional distance and still have trust.

Understanding the Role of Vulnerability in Trust

Vulnerability plays a central role in forging deep connections between partners. It allows individuals to be transparent about their emotions, even when those emotions are messy or uncomfortable. Trust grows not just from the absence of betrayal but from the presence of emotional openness and truth. When partners understand the importance of being vulnerable, they create an atmosphere where both feel accepted as they are. This environment fosters deeper emotional connections, where each person feels seen, valued, and secure.

However, this level of vulnerability can only exist in a relationship where both partners have cultivated self-awareness. When individuals are aware of their emotional triggers, behavioral patterns, and communication tendencies, they can express their feelings more authentically, openly and effectively. In contrast, a lack of awareness can lead to defensiveness, misunderstandings, and conflict, even in the presence of good communication skills.

Understanding How a Lack of Integrity Erodes Trust

Beyond vulnerability, understanding that trust is also built through integrity. Small actions—such as breaking promises, withholding information, or failing to take responsibility for mistakes—can gradually erode trust. Trust isn't just about avoiding major betrayals; it's about showing up consistently, being reliable, and communicating carefully and openly. Keeping your word. A person who frequently engages in dishonest behavior, even in small ways, demonstrates a lack of integrity that slowly chips away at the foundation of trust.

Awareness and understanding are crucial in recognizing how these small behaviors impact the relationship. It requires self-reflection and emotional intelligence to notice when patterns of dishonesty or manipulation are developing and to correct them before they damage the relationship further. When couples cultivate this level of awareness, they can navigate challenges together, address issues honestly, and rebuild trust when it falters.

Self-Awareness is the Foundation of Personal Growth

Self-awareness is the foundation of personal growth and the key to building healthy relationships. Understanding one's thoughts, emotions, and behaviors helps individuals make intentional choices rather than reacting impulsively. Without self-awareness, partners may fall into negative patterns—blaming each other, shutting down emotionally, or engaging in passive-aggressive behaviors. But with self-awareness, they can recognize these tendencies, take responsibility for their actions, and make conscious efforts to improve.

Developing self-awareness is one of life's most rewarding challenges. It requires regular self-reflection, emotional discipline, and a willingness to confront uncomfortable truths about oneself. The more self-aware individuals become, the more they understand how their emotions influence their actions, allowing them to communicate more effectively and nurture healthier relationships.

Building a Strong Foundation through Awareness and Understanding

The importance of awareness and understanding form the foundation of a strong person, and a healthy marriage. They allow couples to navigate the complexities of trust, communication, and emotional connection with greater ease. When partners are aware of their own emotions and behaviors, as well as the needs and perspectives of each other, they can build a relationship based on clarity, respect, empathy, and correct information.

This type of union, one rooted in awareness and understanding, and forged in prayer with and for one another becomes a union without division. More so, communication becomes more than just the exchange of words; it becomes a way to connect, grow, and deepen the bond. With awareness and understanding of how a marriage is supposed to move in harmony, build resilience, and create a relationship that thrives through every season of life.

Awareness and understanding along with prayer are like that hardened bond, when it dries becomes unbreakable. It's like the secret to a lasting marriage (that glue, when applied correctly, heavenly)—not because they eliminate challenges—but because they empower couples to face those challenges together, with empathy, patience, wisdom, and grace. When both partners are committed to growing in awareness and understanding, they create a relationship that is not only strong, also deeply fulfilling, rich in love, trust, and emotional connection. And when both add daily practice and prayer to the foundation it helps them see the other person's well-being rather than focus on themselves.

The power of being self-aware enough to establish habits of prayer and solitude plays a powerful role in developing emotional strength and relational maturity, and a closeness to our heavenly Father. Solitude isn't isolation—it's **intentional time alone** for reflection, understanding, growth, and spiritual grounding. Solitude allows a person to know who they are apart from roles, expectations, or external noise. Consistent prayer creates a desire to connect to God and His righteousness. You become rooted in your core values, which helps you show up authentically in a relationship and in life. You're less likely to lose yourself in someone else's needs or approval when you are following God's plan. Prayer, prayer and more prayer. Let's dive deeper..

Chapter 7
The Power And Impact Of Prayer In Marriage

The awareness to God's presence and the path to seeking God's will is found through a life devoted in prayer

As our Lord and Savior Jesus Christ taught us that when we accept the power of submitting our will to God's will through prayer as an act of the ultimate trust, we invite spiritual transformation. Prayer is the ongoing opportunity to engage deeply with God and one another. This is an act developed with honesty and discipline to persist in seeking His presence in our life — also to be a part of our daily walk with God. It's not about perfection rather connection. Prayer is for edification, affirmation, and communication. It's not about getting what you want, it's about learning how to align your thoughts, your will, and your actions with God. It's about Ask — Seek and Knock through our surrender. Payer is for self examination, petition, and developing a deeper connection with God the Father, God the Son, and God the Holy Spirit.

Ongoing prayer also reveals the healthy patterns of the co-dependency of God in our lives. —DC

This may be the most important chapter in this book to build and practice to sustain a godly relationship within a marriage. Bear with me I don't have much knowledge of the full compass of prayer yet, but much belief in the power and impact it has in forging a bond with you, others and God. The biblical meaning of compass, symbolically, refers to God's order and design and idea of a guiding spiritual path or intention for us. Prayer is one of the deepest and most universal human expressions. At its core, prayer is communication with God—a way of entering into a relationship with Him. By aligning our hearts (minds) with His will, and expressing dependence on Him. It is not only speaking but also listening, not only asking but also receiving, not only an act of faith but also a way of shaping our faith and our character and our spirit.

When both husband and wife decide to cultivate a lifestyle of constant communion with God, choosing an attitude of prayer in their daily life continually turning to God in thought, word, and actions whether when things are good or bad is *paramount* for a godly marriage. And is a living testament to glorify God.

A godly marriage was not designed to be sustainable without understanding, prayer, obedience, and submission. A godly marriage is designed to be under a covenant that calls for spiritual intimacy and understanding of God's purpose for every godly marriage. And one of the most powerful, transformative practices in a God-center marriage is praying for and with your spouse.

Consistent prayer prioritizes and clarifies the unity in marriage to prevent the busyness and selfishness of life that can blind couples of the importance of purpose. Prayer is the spiritual glue that binds a couple together, not just in times of joy or trial, but as a consistent act(glue) of love, compassion, and shared dependence on God.

Praying for your spouse is one of the most intimate and selfless acts of love. When you go before God on behalf of your spouse, you are acknowledging their worth, their struggles and their journey. This is a sincere act demonstrating "I want God's best for you."

Prayer builds compassion, the more you pray for them, the more sensitive you become to their needs. You begin to notice their fears, their battles, and the areas where they need God's Strength and Grace.

Sometimes we try to change our spouse through advice, nagging, or manipulation, even when it's good for them. Prayer is there to do what our words and control never can. It invites the Holy Spirit to do the work. When we are seeking God and desire change in our lives God knows how to transform hearts and minds in ways we cannot. When we pray, we surrender the outcome to God, trusting that He is working even when we don't see it.

While praying for your spouse is powerful, praying with your spouse takes your relationship to another level. Even couples sharing everything—finances, home, parenting, same interests even beds—but never share in prayer. This is a missed opportunity for the deepest form of intimacy: spiritual connection.

When a husband and wife regularly pray together with the same understanding, same submission, same surrender; Wow, something sacred happens. They align themselves with God in a unique way. The bible says that two threads woven together is strength but a third thread becomes a powerful bond. This act allows them to open up their vulnerability before the Lord, and in doing so, they become spiritually naked and unashamed, accepted and empowered. This kind of connection cannot be replicated through any other form of act.

Regularly praying together as a couple creates a special unity. It breaks down walls of offense, softens hearts, and renews understanding. Through good and bad this type of behavior reminds both of the shared foundation—Christ. The practice in regular prayer together keeps the focus away from selfishness and back to servanthood.

This also demonstrates when Jesus said in Matthew 18:19-20, "Again I say to you, if two of you agree on earth about anything they ask, it will be done for them by my Father in heaven. For where two or three are gathered in my name, there I am among them." There is unmatched power in agreement for those who love the Lord, especially between a husband and wife sharing in one vision for God's glory.

More Benefits of a Prayerful Marriage

A union without division requires a prayerful marriage because you understand the purpose and power of doing so.

Here are just a few of the blessings that come from daily prayer in marriage:

1. Deeper emotional bond—Prayer builds trust and opens up for vulnerable opportunities. When we pray expressing our fears, hopes, sins we committed, and with gratitude, it creates a safe space.

2. Increased Forgiveness and Grace—It's difficult to remain bitter or unforgiving when you are consistently praying for and with your spouse. God continues to remind us of humility and compassion.

3. Stronger Spiritual Discernment—When we surrender in prayer we seek God's will not ours for decisions, parenting, finances, ministry, and so on.

4. Deeper Peace and Joy—The presence of God calms anxiety, dispels confusion, and fills the mind and home with peace. A praying couple walks in confidence, peace, and joy in their lives.

First, you don't need to be eloquent. You don't need to be at a certain place in your life. You don't need a perfect script or any experience with a prayer life. You don't need to be well versed. You only need belief, understanding and surrender that depends on God's strength and not yours.

God honors sincerity over sophistication. Begin by setting aside a few minutes each day for yourself and set aside a certain time with your spouse. This time can be in the morning, before bed or a quiet moment together. Just remember the commitment you have with your prayer times the easier it will be for both of you to grow and connect.

Below are some steps to take to create a prayer life, a daily habit:

1. Develop a mind of gratitude—meaning the more grateful we are of God and all that He is the easier it will be to start and maintain these habits. Gratitude, gratitude, and gratitude.

2. Thank God for your spouse every moment you can—start with acknowledging the good things you see in them. And thank them in those moments "use your words." Do this often.

3. Be honest with them about everything, even when it hurts—be transparent when your integrity is in question.

4. Keep your relationship private with your spouse. Unless you are in therapy or counseling.

5. Practice regular intimate moments throughout the day and when you're in a heated conversation or conflict use gentle physical touch is powerful to d—escalate the tension.

6. Practice solitude to build your prayer life and ask for discernment on the areas you need growth. **Work on you not them!**

7. Pray for them daily where they struggle—give mercy, forgiveness, and grace especially when they think they don't deserve it.

8. Ask for strength for your union—seek unity, ask God to help you grow in love, patience, and humility toward each other.

9. Lift up your family—bring your plans before God together, both be in agreement on the direction you are going financially, spiritually, emotionally, ect..

10. Most of all spend time together regularly—sharing about the Kingdom of God and His righteousness for you lives together. Spending time daily could just be 10 or 15 minutes at a time, but often.

A union without division is a union built on godly principles and a foundation of praying. Prayer is the anchor and life-line that keeps us connected to God and spiritually grounded.

The more we pray as a couple it binds us to the unchanging hand to our Lord and Savior through hearing his will for our lives for His glory. This type of prayer life reminds us that marriage is not about us, but about us and God. It's about honoring God, serving one another, and building a legacy of faith and obedience.

When we include solitude as a regular part of our daily activity our prayer life becomes seamless. Solitude with fasting not only opens up our prayer life it is the key ingredient for receiving what God has for us and building that intimate connection. When couples integrate moments and a space of solitude and fasting into their prayer life—it allows them to connect on such a deeper level and maintain focus on their commitment to marriage.

This union without division becomes more than a union—it's a ministry. Let your ministry begin and end with prayer as a habit of the culture we create to bring heaven to earth through us. The godly path to take bringing heaven to earth is incorporating regular moments of solitude in your life. Time alone teaches you how to process emotions internally before reacting, only responding. WWJD (what would Jesus do). You learn to sit with discomfort, understand your triggers, and respond with wisdom. This builds emotional maturity, reducing drama and defensiveness in relationships. In solitude, you reconnect with God (where you can learn to become a spiritual center), gaining peace and direction. You're less likely to place unrealistic demands on your partner for fulfillment. A spiritually grounded person learns to bring stability and vision to the relationship.

When you become aware that solitude contributes to personal accountability and personal growth it forces you to confront your thoughts, choices, and patterns. This awareness awakens your self-honesty and produces growth that benefits the relationship without needing constant affirming or correction from your partner. This type of awareness of how important healthy solitude creates codependency of God's word and reduces independence without distance. You develop the capacity to give and love freely, not from neediness but from overflow. You become more of a contributor, less of a consumer. Your presence adds value rather than drawing energy without giving it. In essence solitude culti-vates inner strength, emotional intelligence, and spiritual depth. These qualities make you a powerful contributor to the health of any relationship—able to love without losing yourself, lead with-out dominating, and connect without clinging. Sometimes we are called to solitude for reflection, discipline, comfort or growth. Let's dive deeper.

Chapter 8
The Quiet Roots That Strengthens Us In Marriage "The Devotion Of Solitude"

Solitude: Fosters Growth

Solitude is often misunderstood or overlooked in the context of building and nurturing personal relationships and intimate relationships. However, it is a fundamental component that allows individuals and couples to deepen their understanding and bond, strengthen their resilience, and foster a space for emotional and spiritual growth. Solitude within oneself and within a relationship is the key ingredient for developing an intimate connection that is both lasting and rooted in purpose. When couples integrate moments and a space of solitude into their relationship, it allows them to reconnect with their spirituality, core values, maintain focus on their commitment, and cultivate acts of understanding, kindness, and service toward themselves and one another.

A relationship built on true intimacy is not dependent on external validation or influenced by the opinions and expectations of the world. Rather, it is a sanctuary that thrives on godly principles, inner strength, and mutual care and respect. This type of relationship does not rely on what society dictates or how the surrounding environment influences behaviors and decisions. Instead, it is grounded in spiritual guidance and mutual devotion that is nurtured in the quiet moments of reflection. Couples who prioritize solitude within their relationship do not spend more time seeking input or validation from friends or external sources than they do with each other and God. They understand that their love and commitment are not meant to be put on display for the approval of others; rather, they seek reassurance and wisdom through the guidance of the Word and in their private, shared moments with their creator.

Solitude enables couples to take the time to pause, reflect, and appreciate the resilience that comes from aligning their relationship with faith-based principles. Spending intentional time in solitude provides both partners with an opportunity to focus on self-awareness and inner strength. It is in these moments that they can reconnect with their individual spiritual journeys and listen to their inner voice, which is often drowned out by the noise of daily life. This inner voice, strengthened by moments of quiet and meditation, empowers couples to remain steadfast in their commitment to each other, no matter the challenges they may face. By stepping away from the constant stream of social media, the opinions of friends, and the influences of the outside world, partners create a disciplined environment that allows them to know themselves and each other more fully.

Maintaining solitude within a relationship helps couples avoid the distractions that can disrupt their focus on each other. The endless information streaming from all directions can make it difficult to stay grounded, but a practice of regular solitude helps quiet the noise and develop a clear sense of purpose. This focus ensures that partners know who they are as individuals and as a couple and reinforces their roles in supporting and loving one another. Solitude enables honest reflection and self-assessment, encouraging partners to rely on their inner truths rather than external feedback. It provides the space needed for growth, where both individuals can process their emotions, build self-awareness, and return to the relationship with renewed energy and clarity.

This type of relationship recognizes that spending time alone, whether individually or as a couple, is not just beneficial but necessary for growth. While it may feel uncomfortable at times not to participate in the social dynamics of friends and networks, this choice empowers couples to develop a deeper appreciation for one another. It nurtures a sense of co-dependence—where partners lean on each other for support and trust—rather than an unhealthy independence that prioritizes outside connections over the relationship itself. Solitude fosters closeness by creating a private, protected space where partners can cultivate their bond without the influence of external opinions. This quiet time together or alone allows them to build a unique and deeply personal fulfillment that transcends societal norms.

One of the main benefits of a relationship focused on intimacy and rooted in solitude is the development of an environment where vulnerability thrives. Solitude encourages partners to express their true selves without fear, leading to a sense of safety and confidence that they are valued for who they are. When couples invest in solitude, they build an emotional bond that emphasizes mutual trust, understanding, and respect. This foundation allows them to explore deeper levels of connection, knowing that they can be open and honest without risking judgment. This type of private intimacy results in a strong desire to know and understand one another on an intrinsic level, enhancing the relationship's stability and resilience.

Solitude fosters an environment that supports both interpersonal and intrapersonal connection. On an individual level, solitude allows each partner to become more self-aware, better understanding their thoughts, emotions, and reactions. This awareness strengthens emotional intelligence and equips them to communicate more effectively and compassionately with their partner. On a relationship level, solitude creates shared experiences of reflection and devotion that are unique to the couple. These moments help build a relationship that does not need external validation to thrive; instead, it is nurtured by the quiet confidence and shared commitment that solitude brings.

By regularly practicing moments of solitude and reflection, couples can build a relationship that is resilient to the pressures of society. It frees them from the expectation to conform to roles that may not align with their personal values or relationship goals. Solitude provides the space needed to break away from stereotypes and create a partnership that is not confined by the opinions of others. This type of relationship is not defined by public displays or the approval of peers but by a deep, private fulfillment that is shared and cherished between partners.

In essence, solitude within oneself and one's relationship serves as an anchor that supports the growth of a meaningful, intimate connection. It encourages partners to cultivate moments of honest reflection and resilience, fostering an atmosphere where love, trust, and understanding flourish. This kind of relationship is not swayed by external distractions or dependent on social validation; instead, it is strengthened by the quiet, intentional acts of devotion and reflection that build a bond rooted in faith, commitment, and true intimacy.

Holy Spirit

Chapter 9
Communication
How To Speak Clearly
And Be Heard

Communication is Only as Effective as Its Understanding

While regular communication is essential, truly understanding enhances the quality and the connection of communication. Awareness of one's own emotions and behaviors, as well as a deep understanding of the other person, allows partners to communicate in ways that are more empathetic and meaningful. Communication is not just about exchanging words or about sharing emotions, it's about understanding the intentions, and experiences.

One of the most profound aspects of communication is the activation of mirror neurons in the brain. These neurons allow individuals to empathize with and mirror the emotions of others. When two people engage in meaningful conversation, their mirror neurons fire in sync, creating a shared emotional experience. This neurobiological process helps couples connect on a subconscious level, deepening their bond. However, the power of these interactions depends on awareness—understanding how emotions influence communication and how to respond empathetically when a partner expresses joy, sadness, or frustration.

The Power of Listening with Awareness

Listening is just as important as speaking and many times more important in a godly marriage. Listening is the root of communication. Active listening requires full attention, empathy, and a willingness to understand the other person's perspective, while acknowledging their value. When partners listen with awareness—without interrupting, judging, or placing expectations on what should be said—they create an environment where each person feels valued and heard.

In contrast, communication can become counterproductive when one partner feels that they are not being listened to. Feeling unheard can lead to frustration, resentment, and emotional withdrawal, which undermines the connection between partners. But when couples take the time to listen actively, they strengthen their emotional bond and foster trust.

Being a good listener is a cornerstone of any relationship, and its significance cannot be overstated. Listening with patience and attentiveness deepens the connection between partners, fostering understanding, trust, and emotional intimacy. It is through active listening that individuals can create a safe space for their partner to express themselves openly, knowing they will be heard, valued, and understood.

When one becomes a good listener, it goes beyond just hearing words; it involves fully engaging with the other person and being present in the moment. Patience is key in this process. A patient listener takes the time to let their partner share their thoughts and feelings without interruption or judgment. This not only encourages open communication but also builds a strong emotional foundation where both individuals feel understood. This level of attentiveness can profoundly influence a partner's behavior by making them feel valued and appreciated, which often inspires reciprocation and more positive interactions.

A critical mindset shift in becoming a good listener is embracing the concept of "listening to speak rather than speaking to listen." Too often, people focus on formulating their response while the other person is talking, missing the essence of what is being shared. A good listener prioritizes understanding over replying. This approach not only enhances the quality of communication but also minimizes misunderstandings and conflicts. By truly focusing on what the partner is expressing, a listener can respond thoughtfully and empathetically, strengthening the relationship.

The benefits of being a good listener start with managing our thoughts and emotions. When we approach conversations with a calm and open mind, we can better control our feelings and respond in a way that nurtures the relationship. Good listening requires self-awareness, as it allows us to set aside personal biases and focus on the needs of our partner. This creates an environment of mutual respect, paving the way for more meaningful communication and affection.

In conclusion, being a good and patient listener is essential for fostering a deep and lasting intimate relationship. It enables partners to connect on a profound emotional level, enhances mutual understanding, and encourages positive behavior. By embracing the principles of active listening, individuals can build a relationship that thrives on trust, respect, intimacy, and love.

Balancing Communication and Emotional Space

While regular communication is essential, there is a delicate balance between healthy conversation and emotional space. Over-communication, particularly when one partner feels pressured to talk excessively or pressured to listen excessively, can lead to being overwhelmed or burnout. Understanding when to give each other space is just as important as knowing when to engage in conversation.

Creating a healthy balance requires awareness of each other's needs and the ability to respect those needs without taking them personally. When both partners feel free to express themselves at their own pace, they are more likely to communicate openly and honestly.

Chapter 10
One Flesh — One Promise When Two Become One Flesh
Chapter 10: Together As One "Marriage"

Many people today believe that a marriage or relationship is about what they can get out of it, which reflects a mindset heavily influenced by individualism and a self-focused culture. Society often equates personal happiness and fulfillment with the success of a relationship, leading individuals to approach partnerships rather than relationships. A modern idea that their partner should primarily contribute to their personal well-being. This belief fosters an attitude, mindset, and environment where individuals focus on their own needs and desires rather than cultivating a marriage of One. Not having a mindset or desire of a shared experience built on mutual understanding and growth of marriage. This is and is not a metaphor for "One Flesh." This is one promise to the other person and for the other person.

The perception that marriage is about individual happiness leads to the idea of "yours" and "mine," rather than "ours." In such relationships, partners may split responsibilities and resources to maintain autonomy, creating an environment where joint lifestyle and shared principles are secondary to personal interests and self gratification. The "I gotta do what's best for me" attitude. Also this attitude expresses "What do you bring to the table?" which fosters an evaluative, transactional approach. Partners might constantly assess each other's contributions instead of appreciating one another and working together to maximize shared beliefs and principles.

This can create a sense of separation within the relationship, as each person feels entitled to what they view as their share and may become resentful if they feel their needs are unmet.

Selfishness within a marriage can be deeply harmful. When one or both partners maintain a self-centered nature, they prioritize their own desires over the well-being of the relationship. This behavior leads to breakdowns in communication, trust, and intimacy. Selfishness erodes the foundation of commitment, love, and communication, as it prevents couples from fully investing in each other and working as a team. The focus shifts from "How can I support you and build a life together?" to "How can I ensure I am getting my fair share?" "I know my worth!" This mindset is a barrier to true connection and prevents partners from nurturing each other through life's challenges. This is not a representation of a godly marriage.

The true blessing and benefit of marriage lie in the commitment to become one—unified in mission, vision, and shared purpose.
—DC

This attitude, mindset, and relationship culture bring us together. Marriage is meant to be a space where two people come together, embracing their unique differences, strengths, and perspectives to create something greater than what they are alone. In this unity, both partners contribute to a shared vision, merging individual interests for collective growth and fulfillment. When a couple shifts their focus from "What's in it for me?" to "How can I enrich my partner's life and share all we have?" the relationship becomes stronger and more resilient. This unity fosters a deep sense of belonging, trust, and emotional security.

Understanding and accepting the inherent differences between men and women—and how these differences complement each other—amplifies the strength of a relationship. Men and women bring varied perspectives, strengths, and emotional approaches that, when respected and harmonized, result in a well-rounded, dynamic oneness. This balance encourages mutual respect and fosters an environment where each partner's unique contributions are valued. Together, these shared efforts create a powerful relationship capable of achieving personal and collective greatness, rooted in love, empathy, and the commitment to grow as one.

Awareness and understanding are especially important when it comes to the differences in how men and women think, behave, and communicate. While both men and women need emotional connection, they often express and receive love differently. Women, by biological and social design, may have a stronger inclination toward nurturing relationships and seeking emotional validation. When this need is met through attentive and affectionate communication, it fosters a sense of security and contentment in the relationship.

Men, on the other hand, may prioritize respect and support as signs of love. They often feel valued when their efforts to provide and protect are acknowledged and appreciated. Understanding these differences helps couples communicate more effectively and meet each other's emotional needs. Without this awareness, misunderstandings can arise, and partners may feel unappreciated or disconnected.

The Role of Empathy in Strengthening Relationships

Empathy is the ability to understand and share the feelings of another person. It is a critical component of awareness and understanding, as it allows partners to connect on a deeper emotional level. Empathy transforms communication from mere words into meaningful connection with interactions that build trust, understanding, and intimacy.

When couples approach each other with empathy, they create a space where both partners feel safe to be vulnerable. They are more likely to respond with compassion rather than criticism, which fosters a sense of emotional security. Empathy also helps couples navigate conflicts by encouraging them to see things from each other's perspectives and work toward mutual understanding.

In conclusion, marriage is not about personal gain but about supporting, caring, and serving a shared life where both partners are better together. Because they are constantly contributing to the other making a stronger union. Shifting the focus from self-centered goals to serving and uplifting one another ensures a relationship thrives on unity, respect, and the pursuit of mutual fulfillment.

Chapter 11
Man's Responsibility
Part 1 of One Flesh
Chapter 11: When a Man Prepares & Increase

Preparing for marriage is one of the most significant journeys a man can undertake. Although most men don't prepare for marriage this may be the most important factor to the health and success of a marriage. At its core, marriage for a man is deciding to undertake a responsibility for his wife and family rooted in love, trust, and sacrifice. This means servitude. While financial stability is often emphasized, the deeper and more critical preparation lies in cultivating one's personal character, developing emotional maturity, and strengthening relational skills. Ironically, when a man begins this journey with little to no financial resources, it often clarifies the importance of these foundational qualities. Starting with nothing allows a man to see what truly matters, pass the provision and develop the essential tools for a successful marriage.

When a man begins his preparation for marriage with an abundance of material wealth, he may unintentionally overlook what is most important: the substance and character of both himself and his potential partner. Wealth can create distractions and even foster superficial desires in the beginning stages, leading to a focus on appearances, possessions, or status rather than the character and spiritual values that sustain a lifelong bond. The danger lies in mistaking material success for readiness, which can obscure the need for emotional intelligence, integrity, and the ability to facilitate a relationship.

In contrast, beginning with little encourages a man to prioritize what money cannot buy. Developing honesty, effective communication, self-respect, and the ability to respect one's partner are far more valuable than any financial asset. I'm not saying financial security is not important, I'm saying men must be mindful of how much money can obscure what is important in relationships. Understanding that the right character traits form the backbone of a strong marriage.

For example, being a good provider isn't solely about financial contributions; it also involves providing emotional security, emotional stability, and providing leadership. A husband must understand the importance of generosity—not just in material terms, but in patience, forgiveness, and empathy. A husband must see God as his seed of generosity and he must be the transfer of that seed of generosity in order to sustain it through the relationship. Forgiveness is another pillar tied to generosity, in particular, is a cornerstone of marriage, allowing both partners to navigate the inevitable conflicts and mistakes with grace and understanding.

Preparation for marriage also requires a man to embrace qualities that reflect true masculinity. Kindness, calmness, and humility are hallmarks of a man ready to lead in marriage. Leadership in this context is not about dominance but about guiding with compassion and with vision. A husband must create a home environment where love and respect thrive, and this begins with his ability to embody these qualities in his daily actions.

Additionally, purpose and planning are critical. A man without a clear sense of direction and purpose has no foundation to offer his marriage. Purpose provides stability and clarity, enabling a husband to support his partner and family through life's challenges. This doesn't mean having every detail figured out but rather having a direction to where he is going, commitment to growth, what are his responsibilities, and how he is to share his goals.

Ultimately, preparing for marriage is about accepting in becoming the best version of oneself. It is about prioritizing the intangible qualities—integrity, humility, compassion, and emotional resilience—that create a meaningful and lasting relationship. While financial stability is important, it should come after these deeper preparations are made. Marriage is not sustained by wealth but by the character and commitment of the people within it. A man who prepares himself in these ways is not just ready for marriage; he is ready to build a life of purpose, appreciation, and enduring love.

These qualities of a man who is prepared to be a good husband are deeply rooted in character, integrity, humility, and a great sense of understanding. A man ready for the commitment of marriage is one who not only meets his responsibilities with humility and dedication, also embodies qualities that bring stability, security, and growth to his family. The readiness to be a husband is about encompassing emotional resilience, moral integrity, spiritual grounding, and a mindset geared toward service and continuous improvement.

Hard Work and Ownership

A man prepared to be a husband takes ownership of his role in providing for himself and his family. This commitment to working hard shows that he understands and respects the value of his role as a provider. He doesn't work hard just for personal gain but recognizes that his efforts contribute to the well-being and security of his family. This man is resilient and persistent, dedicated to facing challenges and ensuring stability. He knows that his commitment to working hard reflects his care for his family and his willingness to invest time and energy into creating a solid foundation for their future.

Such a man demonstrates his preparedness by showing up consistently, regardless of external circumstances. His work ethic and reliability prove his dependability, which is essential for a strong marriage. His actions reveal that he is willing to sacrifice short-term comforts for long-term benefits, reflecting his desire to give his family a life of security and peace.

Servant-Leadership and Humility

One of the core attributes of a prepared husband is the practice of servant-leadership, a concept where he leads through serving others rather than exercising authority over others for self-gain. A good husband is humble, understanding that leadership is not about dominating but about guiding, supporting, and uplifting those around him. His humility enables him to be a better listener, a compassionate partner, and a wise decision-maker. He sees the value in serving his spouse and family, not because he is less but because he understands that genuine strength is expressed through support and sacrifice.

This man leads by example, showing his family how to navigate life with integrity, respect, and steadiness. His actions demonstrate his values, inspiring those around him to embody the same qualities. In every decision he makes, he considers the well-being of his family, aiming to uplift them in ways that encourage growth, happiness, and unity. His humility allows him to continuously grow, accept constructive criticism, and adjust to the needs of his family, ensuring that he remains an effective and compassionate leader.

Accountability and Personal Responsibility

Accountability is one of the cornerstones of a strong marriage for man and woman, and a man prepared to be a good husband understands this deeply. He takes responsibility for his actions, owning his mistakes, learning from them, and making changes when necessary. This level of accountability fosters trust, as his partner knows he is honest and willing to admit his faults rather than deflect blame or hide the truth. His commitment to personal growth strengthens the relationship by creating an environment where both partners feel safe to express themselves openly and work through challenges together.

A husband who is accountable builds a foundation of trust and respect. He acknowledges that everyone has areas for improvement, and he actively works on his weaknesses rather than ignoring them. His willingness to take responsibility reflects his dedication to his marriage, proving that he values his relationship enough to do the work necessary to grow and improve for the sake of his family.

Calmness, Stability, on Purpose

A prepared husband is one who exudes calmness and stability, essential qualities that foster security in a relationship. His composure in the face of adversity reassures his partner and family that they are safe and supported. He is grounded in his sense of purpose and direction, allowing him to make decisions with clarity and confidence. This stability is the backbone of his relationship, providing a consistent, reassuring presence even in turbulent times.

A man with a clear sense of purpose also has a long-term vision for his marriage and family. He sets goals for both himself and his relationship, fostering a shared sense of direction with his partner. His sense of purpose is not self-centered but is rooted in a commitment to building a life that honors his and his family values. By remaining calm and focused, he navigates the ups and downs of marriage with a level-headed approach that keeps him grounded.

Continuous Learning and Personal Growth

Marriage is a relationship that benefits from continuous learning and development. A man prepared to be a husband is eager to learn and develop skills that benefit his family. He knows that self-improvement is an ongoing process, one that enhances his ability to contribute to the well-being of his household. He actively works to improve both hard skills—such as financial management or practical life skills—and soft skills like communication, empathy, and patience. His commitment to self-improvement sets a positive example and reflects his dedication to creating a healthy and nurturing environment for his family.

A husband with this mindset values education and seeks knowledge that can benefit himself and his loved ones. He understands that a well-rounded life includes emotional intelligence, resilience, and adaptability; and much understanding. By investing in his personal growth, he ensures that he remains a strong, positive influence, capable of guiding his family and helping them grow alongside him.

Goal-Oriented and Forward-Thinking

A man prepared for marriage is both goal-oriented and forward-thinking. He doesn't live solely for the present but sets mid- and long-term goals that align with his vision for a stable and fulfilling life. His ability to create and execute plans is a testament to his commitment to ensuring a bright future for his family. This forward-thinking mindset also reflects his dedication to leaving a positive legacy for his children and future generations.

By setting goals, he fosters a sense of purpose and responsibility in his relationship, giving him and his partner something to work toward together. His commitment to his goals demonstrates that he values growth and stability, and he seeks to create a life built on intentionality and shared ambitions. Through his forward-thinking approach, he exemplifies the importance of working toward a greater purpose, ensuring that his marriage is not only fulfilling but also meaningful.

Patience, Kindness, and Selflessness

One of the most important aspects of a prepared husband is his ability to love with patience, kindness, and selflessness. He understands that love is not just a feeling but a set of actions and choices. His patience allows him to listen, support, and nurture his spouse, even during challenging times. He practices kindness, demonstrating compassion and understanding in his interactions. His selflessness is evident in his willingness to put the needs of his family before his own, prioritizing their protection and well-being.

His love is characterized by generosity, as he seeks to give more than he takes, enriching the lives of those he loves. This selflessness reflects a deep respect for his partner and a commitment to fostering a harmonious, caring relationship. His love is enduring, built on the understanding that marriage requires patience, effort, and a willingness to grow together.

Effective Communication and Support

Communication encompasses the whole relationship, and a man prepared for marriage understands the importance of cultivating open and honest dialogue with his partner. He actively works on improving his communication skills, recognizing that clear and compassionate communication is key to resolving conflicts, expressing love, and fostering mutual understanding. He brings more support into the relationship than he demands, ensuring that his partner feels valued and appreciated.

This husband is a supportive partner, always seeking to uplift and encourage his spouse. He offers a steady, compassionate presence, providing comfort and reassurance during difficult times. His ability to communicate effectively and offer support strengthens the bond between him and his partner, creating a relationship rooted in mutual respect, understanding, and shared values.

Honesty, transparency, and Integrity

A man prepared to be a good husband values honesty and integrity above all else. His commitment to truthfulness fosters trust and transparency in his relationship. He not only holds himself to high ethical standards but also encourages and imposes his family to uphold the same values. His integrity is unwavering, and he demands accountability not only from himself but also from those he is responsible for.

This man is reliable and trustworthy, someone his family can depend on. His honesty creates a foundation of trust that makes his relationship strong and resilient. He is steadfast in his principles, never compromising his values for convenience. His dedication to honesty and integrity reflects his commitment to building a marriage based on respect, trust, and shared moral values.

Spirituality and Inner Peace

Finally, a man prepared to be a good husband is centered on a spiritual and moral foundation set by God's standards. His sense of spirituality gives him inner peace and a deeper sense of purpose, allowing him to navigate life with clarity and focus. He understands that true fulfillment comes not from material success but from living a life of meaning, compassion, and service.

His spirituality keeps him grounded, providing him with a source of strength and resilience. He is not consumed by pride or self-centeredness but instead approaches life with humility and gratitude. This foundation of spirituality helps him remain focused on what truly matters, enabling him to be a husband who is not only committed to his family but also to a greater sense of purpose and fulfillment.

In essence, a man who is prepared to be a good husband is one who embraces growth, responsibility, humility, and service. He is a provider, servant-leader, protector, and partner, dedicated to building a life of meaning, stability, and love. His commitment to self-improvement, integrity, and support ensures that his marriage will be grounded in mutual understanding and shared purpose, creating a bond that endures through all of life's challenges. This man is prepared not only to be a good husband but to be a person of true value to everyone around him.

These concepts center on a man who is spiritually prepared for marriage through a deep understanding of his divine purpose, rooted in faith, humility, and a commitment to God's will. To be ready for the role of a husband, he must embody principles that not only drive his personal growth but also empower him to be a source of prosperity and abundance for his future family. This isn't just about financial gain or earthly wealth; it's about true prosperity—a spiritual richness rooted in God's abundance that nurtures everything and everyone in his life.

A husband ready for this role understands his purpose as one of increase—being a source of positive growth for his family, his community, and himself. His focus is on abundance, but not in the sense of hoarding wealth or material success. Instead, he sees prosperity as being aligned with God's will and in harmony with God's purpose for his life. By adopting a philosophy grounded in spiritual wealth rather than just material wealth, he becomes a vessel of divine abundance, living a life that reflects God's goodness and serving as a testament to God's ever-present resourcefulness.

Understanding Prosperity as More Than Material Wealth

This man's understanding of prosperity transcends economic wealth. He sees true prosperity as aligning with God's will and living a life in which he consciously acknowledges God's presence as the ultimate source of all good things. This prosperity manifests not just as personal gain but as an overflow of blessings that he can use to uplift others, guided by his faith. It's about living with an awareness that God's abundance is everywhere and that with faith, he can tap into this divine resource.

This man knows that prosperity in God's will doesn't involve hoarding wealth on earth but investing in heavenly treasures through actions of love, service, and kindness. He lives with a consciousness of God's abundance as a steady, unfailing resource available to him whenever he opens his heart and mind to it. By seeking the goodness of God in all things, he becomes not only prosperous in spirit but also a catalyst for growth and abundance in others' lives.

Building the Foundations of True Spiritual Prosperity

A man with the readiness to be a husband rooted in true prosperity cultivates three core practices:

1. Inclusive relationship with God: He seeks God in all aspects of his life, not only in moments of need. This ongoing relationship is the foundation of his understanding of prosperity.

2. Constant communication with God: Through prayer, meditation, and introspection, he connects with God daily, which strengthens his sense of purpose and direction.

3. Living with a humble spirit: Recognizing his limitations and weaknesses, he allows God to fill him and guide his actions. This is humility in action, a constant reminder that he is a vessel of God's will.

Practical Steps for Achieving Spiritual Prosperity

Now let's examine the practical steps a man can take to develop this type of prosperity—a prosperity based on spiritual growth and alignment with God's will.

1. Daily Devotion and Commitment

For a man to develop a heart ready for increase, he must start with a devoted mindset. This involves:

Setting aside time daily for reflection and devotion: By dedicating time each day to meditate on God's words and his divine purpose, he strengthens his commitment to personal growth.

Transforming commitment into faithful action: This step is about making choices that align with his beliefs. When he commits to something, he does so wholeheartedly until it becomes ingrained in his character.

2. Reading the Word to Seek God's Perception

The Bible and other spiritual texts serve as essential guides for a man aiming to align himself with God's perspective. Practical steps here include:

Regularly reading scripture: He approaches the Word not as a checklist but as a means to deepen his understanding. Regularly reading spiritual self help books and fellowshipping with others sharing a similar walk.

Surrendering personal biases: By recognizing the limitations of his own judgment, he approaches the Word with an open heart, allowing God's truth to shape his views.

3. Being a Lifelong Learner in his Spirituality

Spiritual growth requires a mindset that is always open to learning and a posture of surrender. A man who is willing to learn is humble and acknowledges that his knowledge is limited compared to God's wisdom.

Attending faith-building activities: He actively participates in gatherings, discussions, or retreats that deepen his understanding of God's will.

Seeking mentorship and guidance: He connects with other believers, learning from their experiences and gaining wisdom from those who have walked the path of faith.

4. Adhering to God's Ways Even When Difficult

Following God's ways isn't always easy, especially when they conflict with personal desires or societal norms. This requires:

Practicing obedience: He practices with small challenges and gradually increases his discipline. He learns to follow God's instructions, even when they challenge his understanding or comfort. He understands that he must be obedient even when he doesn't understand why.

Trusting in God's goodness: By believing that God has his best interest at heart, he surrenders his life to divine guidance.

5. Leaning on God's Understanding

A man preparing for the role of husband learns to lean on God's understanding, especially in challenging times.

Turning to prayer in every situation: He seeks God's guidance not only during crises but also in everyday decisions.

Developing resilience through faith: By trusting in God's plan, he cultivates patience and resilience, knowing that God's way is ultimately the best for him.

6. Eliminating Pride

Pride obstructs spiritual growth and is contrary to the humility needed to be a true servant leader in marriage.

Engaging in self-reflection: Regular introspection helps him recognize areas where pride may still linger.

Practicing humility: He makes a conscious effort to put others before himself, especially in his relationship with his spouse.

7. Putting God First in Every Aspect of Life

To be spiritually prosperous, a man must practice putting God at the center of his decisions and interactions.

Inviting God into daily routines: Whether in his work, relationships, or goals, he consciously considers what aligns with God's will.

Seeking God's direction first: Before making significant decisions, he turns to God for guidance, showing that he values divine wisdom above his own.

8. Adapting God's Loves and Hates as His Own

By aligning his values with God's, a man cultivates a heart that genuinely seeks to please God. He loves what God loves and hates what God hates.

Embracing virtues: He practices love, patience, and kindness, traits that God values. He embodies the fruits of the spirits as a way of life.

Rejecting harmful influences: He distances himself from behaviors and attitudes that lead him away from spiritual growth.

9. Practicing "What Would Jesus Do?"

Living with a mindset that emulates Christ's actions instills a deep sense of purpose and alignment with God's will.

Regularly reflecting on Jesus' teachings: He studies the Gospels, considering how he can live out Christ's love and compassion in his own life.

Applying this question in real situations: When faced with moral dilemmas, he asks himself what Jesus would do, choosing to act in ways that align with Christ's example.

10. Finding a Wife Willing to Grow Spiritually

Finally, a man prepared for increase will seek a partner who shares his commitment to spiritual growth, emotional growth, and material growth.

Looking for shared values: He seeks a spouse who is committed to learning and following God's will.

Leading with humility: He doesn't impose his beliefs but instead inspires his wife through his actions, creating a partnership where both individuals grow closer to God.

Conclusion to Part 1

A man ready to be a husband understands that his role involves being a channel of God's abundance—a source of love, strength, provision, and guidance for his family. His understanding of prosperity is rooted in a life aligned with God's purpose, marked by humility, faithfulness, and a commitment to personal growth. Through daily devotion, seeking God's perception, continuous learning, and the willingness to align his values with God's, he cultivates a life that is not only prosperous in spirit but also rich in love, wisdom, and the desire to bless others.

This type of man embodies the qualities of a husband who is prepared to lead a family in faith, rooted in God's abundant love and eternal wisdom. He realizes that true prosperity is not a measure of wealth but a testament to his alignment with God's will—a foundation that will sustain him and his family, leading them toward a life of divine purpose and lasting spiritual wealth.

Chapter 12
Women's Accountability
Part 2 of One Flesh
When A Woman Acquires & Undergo

Becoming a godly wife starts way before she becomes married. This process is under the responsibility and the preparation of the girl's father and mother. A woman raised without a father to guide her or a mother to impart essential values may face unique challenges in becoming a virtuous woman and a valued wife. Without a father, the experience of being a "daddy's girl" may be absent—a role that often helps instill values like respect, understanding, and a sense of self-worth. Similarly, without a mother's teachings, she may lack examples of nurturing, homemaking, or the relationship wisdom that many women traditionally draw upon in their roles as wives.

However, the absence of these influences doesn't mean she cannot grow into the wife God inspires her to be. What is critical is her willingness to acknowledge these gaps and seek growth. This often includes finding a man who is prepared to take on a dual role—both as her partner and as someone who can help guide her in developing the virtues and skills she may not have been taught. For this dynamic to work, she must be willing to submit to the process, not in a sense of losing herself but as an act of trust and creating a relationship to last. Submission here means openness to learning, growth, and embracing accountability. She must be careful because this role isn't for any man, but a godly man.

Submission does not make her less valuable; rather, it reflects her strength and determination to build a life of meaning and purpose and to be accountable to that man as her husband. A man in this role must possess patience, wisdom, and a willingness to lead with humility and love. His guidance should come from a place of respect and genuine care, helping her to cultivate virtues such as respect for herself and others, a strong moral compass, and the relational skills necessary to thrive in marriage.

For this relationship to succeed, mutual commitment is essential. She must be willing to learn, and he must be willing to teach, but both must remain respectful in value and dignity. Together, they can create a relationship that not only fills the void of what was missing in her upbringing but also fosters an environment of love, growth, and mutual respect. This kind of partnership is a testament to the power of humility and shared purpose, enabling both to flourish as individuals and as a couple.

The journey of a woman acquiring herself for wifehood involves much more than preparing for a wedding or adjusting to married life. It is about embracing qualities and commitments that nurture and honor the relationship she will have with her husband. This woman embodies respect, vulnerability, trust, submission, and self-awareness as she steps into a role that values unity, growth, and mutual support.

Submission and Strength Through Trust

At the heart of a woman's readiness to be a wife lies her ability to submit, but not in a way that compromises her sense of self. For this woman, understanding submission is a strength, a conscious decision to trust and support her husband as the leader in their shared journey. She chooses a husband she respects deeply, can easily be vulnerable with, one she can honor and truly believe in. If she can't submit to this man then she is not ready because he is not the one. She needs to find a man she can submit and trust. She must find a man she wants to submit fully to, not to lose her identity or voice; instead, it is a willingness to yield in support of a greater shared purpose and vision for their life together under his leadership.

When a woman truly trusts and believes in her husband, submission becomes a natural and empowering choice. This trust allows her to be vulnerable, which fosters a safe space for her to express her true self without fear of judgment or rejection. In marriage, this vulnerability becomes a powerful tool for emotional intimacy, where both partners feel valued and understood. Her submission reflects her strength because she has chosen a partner who values and respects her, allowing her to surrender to increase herself.

Building Together with a Shared Vision

A woman ready for marriage does not seek individual fulfillment alone; she desires to build a life together with her partner. This woman values mutual goals and strives for a relationship that goes beyond material needs or fleeting desires. She respects her husband's leadership and is committed to fostering a shared vision for their future. Together, they create goals that honor both their individual aspirations and their collective purpose, allowing them to build a meaningful life.

For this woman, building a shared life involves more than just setting goals; it is about cultivating values and principles that guide their choices together. She sees marriage as an ongoing longing, a union that blends her strengths with her husband's, and she recognizes that cooperation in their union will bring fulfillment. Her role in this journey includes supporting her husband's vision while also contributing her unique perspective and skills. She understands that the journey of building a life together requires understanding, patience, and unwavering commitment to the relationship. She knows her happiness cannot oversee him.

Respect for Her Husband's Role and Responsibility

A woman who prepares for marriage has a deep respect for her husband's and his role as a provider, protector, and cultivator. She does not take his efforts for granted but acknowledges and values his dedication to her well-being and to their family's security. She recognizes that her husband's role brings with it responsibilities that he fulfills out of love, care, and commitment. In response, she brings a spirit of gratitude and encouragement, fostering a supportive and nurturing environment for him.

This respect manifests in how she treats him daily. She listens to his ideas and instructions, invites his perspective, and appreciates the sacrifices he makes for their family daily. By respecting his role, she demonstrates her faith in him and in God, which gives him the strength to continue leading and supporting their family with confidence and love. Her respect for his role also means she refrains from criticizing or undermining him, especially in front of others. Instead, she speaks fondly of him and avoids discussing private matters behind his back, choosing to preserve his dignity and honor their relationship.

Commitment to Serve and Sacrifice

A woman prepared to be a wife embodies a spirit of servitude and sacrifice. She sees her role in the marriage as one of service—not out of obligation, but out of love and devotion to him and her family. This woman is aware and with the understanding that marriage requires putting others' needs before her own at times, as a gesture of love and commitment. Her willingness to serve is not rooted in submissiveness or inferiority but in a heartfelt desire to contribute positively to her husband and family's well-being.

This type of service goes beyond household duties; it extends into emotional, physical, and spiritual support. She is there for her husband, offering comfort, encouragement, and empathy when he faces challenges. Her sacrifices reflect her understanding that love sometimes requires prioritizing her partner's needs or supporting him in his dreams and aspirations. Her commitment to serve is a gift of love and dedication that builds a foundation of trust and respect in their marriage.

Following Her Husband's Lead with Faith and Trust

This woman willingly follows her husband as he leads, not because she cannot lead herself but because she has chosen a man whose guidance she trusts to lead her who she respects, and she believes this is what is right in marriage. Her faith in his leadership is grounded in her belief that he is a man of integrity and honor who loves her and God; and has her best interests at heart. She knows that by submitting to his leadership, she is empowering him to take on his God-given role as the head of the household, a role she supports with her own unique strengths and beliefs.

Her decision to follow his lead does not diminish her value; rather, it unifies their purpose and strengthens their relationship. She views his leadership as a way to maintain harmony and direction in their marriage, allowing both to contribute meaningfully to their shared vision. Her trust in his leadership gives him confidence, and her faith in his abilities inspires him to lead with integrity, humility, and wisdom.

Pleasing Her Husband Through Pleasing God

For this woman, being a good wife means being a godly wife. Aligning her actions with a higher purpose. She is motivated by a desire to please her husband, but ultimately, her true purpose is to please God. She views her role as a wife as a divine calling, an opportunity to live out her faith by serving her husband with love, humility, and grace. By focusing on her spiritual growth and alignment with God, she finds the strength and wisdom to support her husband in a way that honors her commitment to both her marriage and her faith.

Her relationship with God provides her with guidance, patience, and a deep sense of purpose. She is not concerned with perfection but rather with striving to embody the virtues that bring her closer to God and closer to her husband. Through her devotion to God, she finds joy and fulfillment in serving her husband, knowing that her role in their marriage is part of a greater plan.

Acceptance and Appreciation of Her Husband's Imperfections

A woman who is ready for marriage does not seek to change her husband. She understands that marriage is not about molding her partner into a version of her own ideal but about accepting him as he is. She believes her marriage is about praying, supporting, and feeding back into him for his growth. She understands that marriage is not about controlling her partner or every aspect of the relationship. She understands that marriage is not about things always going her way or "happy wife happy life." She values his strengths, appreciates his unique qualities, and embraces his imperfections. This acceptance does not mean she condones harmful behavior, but rather that she does not dwell on superficial flaws or shortcomings. She corrects or guides him if he strays from the values they both hold, especially those rooted in their faith, but she does so with love and respect.

Her acceptance fosters an environment where her husband feels secure, valued, and loved. By appreciating him as he is, she builds a marriage that is free from the constant pressure of unrealistic expectations. Her love is not conditional on his perfection but is rooted in a deep respect for his character and his dedication to their shared life.

Expressing Gratitude and Avoiding Demeaning Criticism

Gratitude is a central pillar of a healthy and loving marriage, and a woman prepared to be a wife practices gratitude consistently. She expresses sincere appreciation when her husband goes out of his way to support her or make her feel valued. She even expresses her appreciation when her husband just does the small things in their everyday life. By showing gratitude, she reinforces the bond between them, letting him know that his efforts do not go unnoticed. Her appreciation encourages him to continue nurturing their relationship, creating a positive cycle of love, support, and acknowledgment.

She avoids demeaning him or making him feel inadequate, especially for things he may not be able to provide. Instead of focusing on what might be lacking, she values his strengths and his commitment to their family. By choosing not to criticize or belittle him, she fosters a loving environment where both partners feel safe and respected. Her respect for him creates a foundation where he feels empowered to give his best, knowing that his efforts are valued.

Valuing His Perspective and Showing Respect Publicly and Privately

A woman who is prepared to be a wife respects her husband's perspective, even if it differs from her own. She values his insight and is willing to listen, understanding that different viewpoints can enrich their relationship. She does not dismiss his ideas or override his opinions but considers them with an open heart and mind. This respect for his perspective reflects her commitment to maintaining harmony and mutual understanding.

Respect extends beyond private conversations; it is equally important in public. She speaks highly of him around friends and family, choosing to honor their relationship by avoiding negative comments or mockery. She does not discuss his shortcomings with others or make fun of him in a way that could damage his dignity. Her commitment to showing respect, both publicly and privately, reinforces her loyalty and builds a foundation of trust and admiration.

Cultivating a Loving and Nurturing Home Environment

A woman who prepares herself for marriage understands the importance of setting a positive tone in her home. She recognizes that a loving, welcoming atmosphere is vital for a thriving marriage, and she takes it upon herself to cultivate this environment. She nurtures her home with kindness, warmth, patience, self-control, and gentleness creating a space where both she and her husband feel comfortable and at peace.

Even when she may not feel her best, she chooses to approach her role with kindness and grace. Her commitment to maintaining a healthy, affectionate relationship invites harmony and joy into their home. She sets the tone by fostering an environment where love and respect are always present and moving about freely, creating a foundation for a strong, lasting marriage.

A Wife Who Honors, Submits, and Serves Through Love

Ultimately, a woman prepared to be a wife embodies a heart that honors, submits, and serves through love. Her role is not one of obligation but of genuine dedication to her husband, her family, and her faith. She is a wife after God's heart, a partner who aligns her actions and intentions with values that honor her marriage and her spiritual journey even in the times when her husband doesn't.

Her love is enduring, selfless, and committed

A woman who understands her accountability to both her husband and God embraces a sacred role in marriage. Her commitment is not just to her spouse but to fulfilling a divine calling. She embodies a spirit of service, humility, and dedication to her husband's growth and well-being while staying rooted in her faith and her responsibility to God. This type of wife aligns herself with the principles of a godly woman as described in Scripture, seeking to be a "help meet"—a partner who supports, uplifts, and nurtures her husband's purpose as an extension of God's design for marriage.

This virtuous woman doesn't see her role as limited to the practical aspects of marriage; she views it as a spiritual mission. Her life, attitude, and actions serve to glorify God and embody the divine purpose for which marriage was created. She takes on this role selflessly, not seeking personal gain or validation, but dedicating herself to the forward movement of her husband's purpose and the growth of their shared life together. This requires a balance of strength and humility, faith and service, and a deep understanding of her role as a wife who is called to support and nurture without undermining or overpowering. Wow!

Understanding the Role of a Godly Wife

The role of a godly wife is one of intentionality, love, and respect. She understands that:

Marriage is a relationship of purpose, rooted in mutual submission, trust, and faith.

Her role is to be a help meet: This term, rooted in Scripture, signifies a partner who actively supports, uplifts, and aids her husband. This godly wife has chosen to live a life of one shared vision with her husband.

Submission is an act of strength and love: Far from diminishing her, submission is a powerful, active choice to align with God's design for the marriage.

She is entrusted with nurturing her family: This includes her husband, children, and even her wider circle, all of whom benefit from her presence and influence.

Her life is about glorifying God: She recognizes that her ultimate purpose is to honor God through her marriage, creating a union that reflects His love, patience, and strength.

In fulfilling this role, the godly wife is a steward of her husband's well-being, a nurturer of her family's growth, and a keeper of her home's spiritual atmosphere.

This accountability requires virtues such as patience, humility, and unwavering faith. Such a woman strives to become a source of encouragement and stability, a partner who contributes positively to the growth and health of her relationship. Her focus is on fostering an environment of love, understanding, and faith, all while maintaining her commitment to God's will.

Practical Steps for a Woman to Achieve Virtue and Faithfulness

Becoming this virtuous and faithful wife involves a set of practical steps rooted in daily devotion, a nurturing spirit, and a commitment to living in alignment with God's design.

1. Daily Devotion and Commitment to Transformation

To be a truly nurturing and encouraging wife, a woman must first cultivate a life of daily devotion. This transforms her from within and aligns her actions with her faith.

Setting time for prayer and reflection each day: Through prayer and devotion, she builds a foundation of faith that strengthens her commitment to her role.

Engaging in practices that reinforce her dedication: By consistently nurturing her mind and spirit, practicing healthy emotional behaviors, she transforms daily routines into moments of spiritual growth.

Being mindful in her interactions with her husband: This involves showing patience, kindness, and encouragement, even during challenging times.

2. Reading the Word to Seek God's Perception

This step involves setting aside personal desires to focus on what God wants for the marriage. A godly wife reads Scripture not only for wisdom but to align her actions with God's perception.

Reading with a spirit of openness: Instead of seeking validation for her desires, she asks God to reveal His will for her life and in her marriage.

Putting her husband's needs before her own:

In a godly marriage, a wife who understands her accountability to both her husband and God plays a pivotal role. She recognizes that her position as a wife isn't about companionship or partnership but about fulfilling the call of a wife that chooses this role in her life. Her presence is essential for fostering an environment of growth, stability, and spiritual richness within the marriage. This kind of woman embraces her role as a "help meet," a term rooted in biblical teachings that signifies a partner who complements and supports her husband's life, purpose, and spiritual journey. She is willing to be submissive as an expression of her strength, humility, and commitment to God's design for marriage.

This woman's main approach to marriage is not driven by self-interest or material gain but by a commitment to being a blessing to her husband, just like a "gift." She understands that her role is to glorify God by helping her husband fulfill his purpose and nurturing the growth of everyone around her. She is a selfless woman, refraining from putting undue pressure on her husband to provide things beyond his means or expecting him to be someone he is not. Instead, she focuses on creating a safe, nurturing environment where he can thrive, and she adapts to support what is given to her, making the most of their shared resources for the benefit of the family.

Understanding the Role of a Godly Wife

For a godly wife, the role she plays in marriage is multifaceted and deeply spiritual. She understands that:

1. Marriage is a Divine Union: The purpose of marriage goes beyond personal fulfillment; it is designed by God to reflect His love and grace. By taking her role seriously, she honors this design.

2. A Help Meet: She sees herself as her husband's support system, aligning with his goals and encouraging his growth. "Help meet"

implies partner but also carries the connotation of active support that enables her husband to fulfill his purpose.

3. Submissive Yet Powerful: Submission in marriage is often misunderstood, but for this woman, it means exercising her strength in a way that complements her husband's leadership, contributing to the health of the relationship.

4. Focused on Nurturing: Her role involves cultivating an environment that promotes emotional, spiritual, and physical well-being. Her nurturing presence is a gift that sustains the household and makes it a place of refuge and growth.

5. Selflessness and Accountability: She operates from a place of selflessness, always considering the bigger picture and placing her relationship with God above worldly desires.

Practical Steps to Develop Virtue and Faithfulness

A woman can become this virtuous and faithful wife through intentional steps that deepen her commitment, strengthen her character, and align her with God's purpose for her marriage. Here are ten practical steps toward this goal.

1. Daily Devotion and Commitment of the Mind

Devotion is the foundation for a godly wife, grounding her actions in faith and dedication. A wife that influences and promotes prayer time with her husband daily. A wife who prays over her husband and family regularly.

Setting Aside Time for Prayer and Meditation: Daily prayer connects her to God and allows her to approach her marriage with humility and strength. Through prayer, she gains wisdom and grace to handle challenges.

Transforming Her Commitment into Action: True devotion goes beyond words and transforms into action. She nurtures her husband through small gestures of kindness, encouragement, and support, making her commitment tangible. Always willing and ready to cooperate even through the difficult times.

Mindful Encouragement: She focuses on being a source of support, offering encouragement and positive reinforcement to her husband, which helps him grow in his faith and purpose.

2. Seeking God's Perception Over Her Own Desires
A godly wife strives to see her marriage through God's eyes, allowing His perspective to guide her actions.

Studying Scripture Regularly: By immersing herself in God's Word, she gains insight into His intentions for marriage, which empowers her to set aside personal desires and focus on her husband's needs.

Prioritizing Her Husband's Needs: Acknowledging her role as a help meet, she willingly puts her husband's vision before her own, creating a supportive and harmonious relationship.

3. Embracing a Teachable Spirit

A godly wife maintains a posture of learning and adapting, especially in matters of faith and marriage. Willing and ready to adapt to the direction of her husband.

Learning to Listen First: She practices listening as a foundation for communication, valuing her husband's input and ideas.

Adhering to Her Husband's Leadership: By respecting his role as the leader of the household, she fosters unity and encourages him to embrace his responsibilities.

Continually Seeking Spiritual Growth: She remains open to learning and growth, knowing that her strength comes from God and that spiritual maturity enhances her role as a wife.

4. Following God's Ways Even When They're Challenging
Living according to God's will sometimes requires sacrifice and endurance, especially when it conflicts with personal desires.

Demonstrating Faith Through Actions: She exemplifies her beliefs through her lifestyle, not only for her husband's benefit but also as a role model for her children and community.

Teaching God's Ways Through Example: By living a life of faith and obedience, she teaches her children and others to follow God's path.

5. Living a Life of Forgiveness and Compassion
Forgiveness and compassion are vital in any relationship, and a godly wife practices these virtues daily.

Choosing to Forgive Freely: She recognizes that holding onto resentment harms the marriage, so she forgives easily, understanding that forgiveness brings healing and peace.

Cultivating a Compassionate Heart: She approaches her husband's challenges with compassion, offering understanding and support without judgment.

6. Looking Beyond Today's Needs

A godly wife sees the bigger picture and does not base her happiness solely on immediate gratification.

Practicing Patience and Long-term Thinking: She understands that marriage is a journey and is willing to wait, sacrificing temporary comfort for lasting growth.

Avoiding Emotional Dependency: She doesn't rely on her husband alone for emotional fulfillment but finds peace in her relationship with God, which enables her to support her husband with a clear mind and open heart.

7. Prioritizing God Above All Else

A wife who puts God first creates a strong foundation for her marriage and her own well-being.

Daily Prayer and Reflection: By putting God at the center of her life, she gains the strength to handle marriage challenges with grace.

Finding Peace in God: Instead of relying solely on her husband for emotional support, she finds a deep and unshakeable peace in her relationship with God.

8. Aligning Her Heart with God's Values

The godly wife seeks to align her heart and actions with what God loves, rejecting things that don't reflect His character.

Embracing Godly Values: She incorporates qualities like kindness, patience, and humility, which mirror God's nature and create a nurturing environment for her family.

Rejecting Harmful Influences: She avoids behaviors or attitudes that could bring harm or discord into her marriage, focusing on creating a loving and peaceful atmosphere.

9. Viewing Marriage as a Divine Union

A godly wife sees her marriage not just as a partnership but as a union designed to glorify God and honor her husband.

Honoring the Sacredness of Marriage: She views her role as a wife as a calling, seeing her actions as contributing to a larger purpose beyond herself.

Embracing Unity: She works to create a bond with her husband that reflects God's intention for marriage, fostering unity, respect, and love.

10. Seeking a Husband Who Can Lead Spiritually

The choice of a spouse is crucial. A godly wife seeks a husband who she shares his commitment to spiritual growth. Choosing a Husband Who Honors God: She values qualities like integrity, faithfulness, and spiritual strength, recognizing that these traits make a man suitable to lead the family.

Encouraging Her Husband's Spiritual Growth: She supports her husband in his own faith journey, knowing that his spiritual strength will benefit the entire family.

Conclusion to Part 2
Becoming a Woman of Virtue and Faithfulness

A virtuous woman embodies qualities of humility, strength, and devotion. She is both a supporter and an active participant in her marriage, ensuring that her home is a place of peace, growth, and godly influence. She leads through service and example, creating an environment that reflects the love, patience, and wisdom of God. This type of woman doesn't seek validation through material possessions or social status but finds joy in being a blessing to others, continually seeking spiritual growth and fulfillment through her relationship with God.

Through daily devotion, a commitment to seeing her marriage through God's perspective, and a willingness to learn and adapt, this woman becomes a beacon of virtue and faithfulness. Her submission to her husband is an expression of her devotion to God, and her nurturing spirit strengthens the bond within her family. Ultimately, a godly wife serves not only her husband and family but also glorifies God by fulfilling the purpose for which marriage was created. This is a high calling and a role that she embraces wholeheartedly, with conviction and grace, creating a marriage that reflects God's love and serves as an example to others.

In her journey, she grows in emotional maturity, she grows in spiritual maturity, drawing closer to God, which in turn enhances her ability to be a loving, faithful, and virtuous wife. This foundation ensures a stable, healthy, and fulfilling relationship that stands as a testament to God's design for marriage—for a union without division. When responsibility and accountability are answered in the roles of man and woman—within a godly relationship forged in honesty.

A union without division when you both are ready for marriage.

CHAPTER 13
WHEN YOU BOTH KNOW IT'S GOD'S MARRIAGE
We Know!

"I realized the first time I saw her I knew."

"I knew when I couldn't go a day without talking to him he was the one."

"I knew because I felt I wanted to be with him forever."

"I knew because we just fit, he would finish my sentence, he knew the things I liked, he even knew when I was cold he would just bring me a blanket."

"I knew he was the one when I no longer feared being alone."

"I knew because when I'm with her it feels like home."

"I knew I was with my one because I just ended a broken relationship and when he came into my life I felt comfortable and secure almost like I was finally healed."

"I knew I met the one when I no longer had to worry about fixing me or working on myself because he accepted me for who I am."

"I knew I met my one, because we communicate so well. We talked for hours and hours and I finally felt understood."

"I knew I met the one because I felt an immediate sense of peace after meeting him. It was like our souls were connected."

None of these examples given above are examples that you know. You are only feeling some chemistry or connection behind some shared experiences. Many times the feelings people describe are a beautiful reflection of chemistry and emotional connection, the kind of bond that can feel magnetic and life-changing. It's a rare and special moment when you meet someone who seems to fit you so effortlessly.

These moments of recognition—the way they bring you a blanket without asking, the ease with which conversations flow, and the sense of comfort and security—are powerful signs of compatibility. It feels like your soul has found a companion, someone who makes life lighter, brighter, and full of promise.

However, it's important to remember that while chemistry and emotional connection is an essential part of any relationship, it doesn't define nor are essential part of the foundation of a Godly marriage, nor will it sustain any relationship. Chemistry is emotional and instinctive, often based on feelings and immediate connections, while a Godly marriage requires intentionality, spiritual alignment, and a commitment that transcends emotions.

In a Godly marriage, love is patient, sacrificial, and enduring. It thrives not just on the warmth of shared moments but also on the hard work of building a life together rooted in faith, trust, and mutual growth. It calls for both partners to support each other's spiritual journeys, to forgive, and to put God at the center of their relationship.

While chemistry can spark a relationship, it's the deeper foundation of shared values, purpose, and reliance on God that sustains it. A Godly marriage is less about "fixing" one another or feeling "complete" and more about walking together, fully aware of your individual imperfections, united in love, forgiveness and a shared promise to God's plan. That peace and security you feel can deepen and transform when anchored in God's love and guidance.

The Pathway to A Union Without Division — Putting God First

THIS IS WHEN YOU KNOW IT'S GOD'S MARRIAGE

When your marriage is under the covenant of God's love, something sacred happens—you become vulnerable. You become willing to open yourself fully to the other, no longer protecting yourself from the very one you vowed to trust. In this place, there is no defense—there is only **surrender**.

Marriage was not built for competition, but built for surrender to a union without division. —DC

Covenant love is not natural. Yes, covenant love is **not natural**—it must be learned, practiced, and many times fought for and strengthened in the presence of God. The easy seasons of marriage are not proof of God's presence, and the hard seasons are not evidence of failure. The difficult seasons are the **training ground** where covenant grows deeper roots.

Every marriage goes through difficulties. Every couple walks through personal struggles, frustration, and disappointment. Every union faces storms. Difficulty does not mean defeat—it means you are living in an ever-changing world that will always present challenges. Yet many of the influences of this world work overtime to convince couples that struggle means it's time for separation.

But in God's Word, struggle is the **soil** where perseverance, compassion, humility, and unity grow.

What breaks marriages is not hardship—it is **selfishness and separation**. It is **not pain**, but **hopelessness**, that begins to creep in. When couples lose sight of God's design, they begin to assume that struggle means God has abandoned them, or that the relationship no longer works. In truth, many times struggle and pain are signals that God is strengthening what was weak, rebuilding what was cracked, and realigning what drifted out of order.

The vows spoken at the altar are often quickly forgotten under pressure, pain, loss, and compromise. When unmet expectations appear, our focus shifts. In today's generation, many enter marriage as if it were easily breakable—because they enter it as a **con-**

tract. And contracts were never strong enough to carry the weight of two imperfect people.

In a marriage contract love is conditional, values are monetary, visual appearances are part of the long-term conditions, behavior determines loyalty, performance determines worth failure becomes a foreseeable doorway to the future of escape.

But God's marriage is not based on emotion, behavior, or conditions. It is based on a **promise**—a commitment that does not depend on how we feel, how we act, or what we have. God's marriage operates on **covenant love**, the same structure that holds together His relationship with humanity.

This covenant is not based on happiness, emotions, or desire—it is based on **promise**. Covenant depends on what we vowed **in the presence of God** on the day we joined our lives together.

This covenant means:
- I choose you even when you don't choose me.
- I love you even when it costs me something.
- I will submit even when I don't feel like it.
- I will cherish you even when you disrespect me or take my love for granted.
- I am yours in the good, the bad, and even the unholy times.

It means a union without division.
It means what God has joined together, let no man separate.

And this should remind us—marriage is not held together by compromise or compatibility. It is held together by **covenant**.

Marriage, especially a Godly one, is a profound union that transcends mere companionship. It reflects God's covenant with His people and serves as an avenue to glorify Him through love, submission, and surrender. The readiness for such a sacred bond goes beyond emotional affection or societal pressure; it necessitates deep spiritual preparation, maturity, and alignment with God's principles. Below, I will expand on the qualities and milestones that indicate readiness for a Godly marriage.

1. Centered on God's Principles and Righteousness

The foundation of a Godly marriage begins with a life firmly rooted in God's principles. When you have chosen to live a life that pleases God, it shows in your daily choices, behaviors, and values. You are not swayed by fleeting trends or societal expectations but by an unwavering commitment to righteousness. You understand that marriage is a lifelong covenant and wish to share your journey of faith with someone who is equally devoted to God. When this alignment with His ways feels natural and fulfilling, it's a clear sign of readiness.

2. Trusting God's Plan Completely

Readiness for a Godly marriage requires trust in God's sovereignty, even when His ways are not easily understood. Even when His ways are not easy or accepted by others. This trust manifests in faithfulness to His will, prioritizing His plan over personal desires.

You recognize that God's timing, methods, and choices are perfect, and you're willing to wait or make sacrifices as needed. This trust ensures that your marriage will be built on a solid foundation of faith, making you ready to face life's uncertainties with a partner who shares the same belief.

3. Alignment with God's Desires

When you know you are in or ready for a Godly marriage involves aligning your heart with God's heart—loving what He loves and hating what He hates. This process requires intentional learning and self-reflection. By immersing yourself in His Word and actively applying it, you develop a character that reflects God's values. This alignment allows you to approach marriage with a pure heart, ready to love and serve your partner in a way that honors God, not your old self.

4. Security in God's Plan

Living within God's plan brings a sense of safety and security. This assurance is not rooted in worldly guarantees but in a deep relationship with God. When you are prepared for a Godly marriage, your primary concern becomes living a life that pleases Him, just as a child strives not to disappoint a loving parent. This fear is not about punishment but about reverence and love. Such a perspective fosters a sense of responsibility and devotion that is essential for a marriage rooted in faith.

5. Preparedness for Marriage's Demands

Marriage is a spiritual promise, a commitment that requires discipline, mindfulness, respect, care, and thoughtfulness. Readiness for a Godly marriage means you've spent significant time preparing yourself emotionally, spiritually, and practically. This preparation includes learning to navigate challenges, developing patience, and cultivating a servant-hearted attitude. By committing to personal growth, you position yourself to be a helpful and supportive partner, especially during difficult times.

6. Understanding Biblical Roles in Marriage

Godly marriage involves fulfilling roles as defined by Scripture. Husbands are called to love their wives sacrificially, as Christ loves the Church, while wives are called to submit in love and respect. This mutual submission under God's covenant ensures a balanced, harmonious relationship. When you have studied and embraced these roles, understanding their spiritual significance and practical application, you are prepared to enter a lifelong commitment that glorifies God.

7. Mastery of Healthy Communication

Effective communication is crucial for any successful relationship, especially a marriage rooted in faith. Readiness for a Godly marriage includes the ability to listen more than you speak, fostering understanding and connection. This involves practicing empathy, patience, and humility in conversations. By mastering these skills, you create a safe and nurturing environment where both partners feel heard and valued.

8. Possessing Essential Relationship Qualities

Certain qualities are indispensable for a Godly marriage: honesty, respect, forgiveness, generosity, and an intimate relationship with God. These traits form the bedrock of a healthy, enduring union. When you consistently demonstrate these qualities in your daily interactions and relationships, it is a strong indicator that you are ready to embody them in marriage.

9. A Selfless Approach to Marriage

When you are ready for a Godly marriage it is not about seeking personal gain but about serving your partner selflessly. When you are more invested in the relationship's well-being than your own comfort, you display the humility and sacrificial love that mirrors Christ's love for the Church. This selflessness ensures that you approach marriage with the intention of giving, supporting, and uplifting your spouse, regardless of their contributions.

10. A Positive and Contagious Attitude

A cheerful heart and positive outlook are vital for building a joyful marriage. Readiness for a Godly marriage means you've cultivated a habit of inviting laughter, smiles, and optimism into your life. This positivity not only enriches your own well-being but also enhances your partner's experience in the relationship. When both individuals bring such an attitude to the union, it creates an environment of mutual encouragement and delight.

The Confidence to Commit

When these qualities are evident in your life, you can approach marriage with confidence and assurance. You are ready. You recognize that marriage is not about perfection but about two individuals growing separately yet together in Christ. By embodying these principles, you set the stage for a union that reflects God's glory, serves His purpose, and stands the test of time.

In conclusion, readiness for a Godly marriage is not a destination but a journey of preparation, surrender and growth. It requires intentionality, humility, and a deep relationship with God. When you can look at your life and see these markers of spiritual maturity, selflessness, and alignment with God's will, you can be assured that you are ready to embark on this sacred covenant.

When two people realize they are deeply submitting to one another, they find themselves in a relationship that is not only fulfilling but also grounded in a deep sense of purpose, mutual respect, and shared beliefs. Spiritual compatibility, in this sense, goes far beyond superficial qualities or shared hobbies. It reaches into the core of their lives, aligning their values, principles, and understanding of a higher purpose. This deep connection becomes a source of immense gratitude, as they recognize that what they share is rare and precious. For such a couple, compatibility isn't just about getting along—it's about becoming an anchor for one another, a reflection of mutual respect, shared values, and a harmonious vision for the future.

When your marriage is under the covenant of God's love, self-protection ends and **surrender begins**. God's marriage is not built on competition—it is built for **a union without division**. Let's discover how this looks when you put God first in the next chapter.

Chapter 14
PUT GOD FIRST
The War For The Throne
Union without division — this is where it all begins

Deep down have you ever said how do I put God, and had no idea what it truly meant. What does this really mean? Do I lose who I am? Do I get to keep my personality? Do I need to lose the things I really like about who I am? What it means is no more excuses, no divided heart, many may not agree with this but when they really understand what it means to fear God, they will. This means I don't want to disappoint My Father who is in heaven.

PUTTING GOD FIRST: THE WAR FOR THE THRONE

To put God first in your life means understanding one unshakable truth: **God does not share His throne.** If you truly place Him there, you will discover the security, peace, and joy you were created for. But this does not mean life suddenly becomes easy or painless. In fact, it means the opposite.

Prepare yourself for struggle—especially as you draw closer to complete surrender.

Only those who rest in the One who cannot be moved will experience what happens next. Something supernatural begins to unfold. Worries shrink. Desires are purified. Priorities realign. When the Kingdom of God comes first, everything else finds its proper place. God does not bless leftovers.

He will not squeeze Himself into the cracks of your calendar or stand in line behind your other priorities. He is not a weekend accessory. **He is King.**

That truth is threatening to most of us. Our hearts are often divided. We want God's blessings, yet we cling tightly to our own kingdoms. We invite Him to rule only when life becomes unbearable, attempting to split the throne—but God will never accept that arrangement. He will not bow to our idols, our convenience, or our way.

And because He loves you, He will tear them down—even when it breaks your heart.

You were designed to worship Him first. That is the architecture of your soul. Anything else placed in that position—career, relationships, money, health—will eventually collapse under the weight of your expectations. Only the Kingdom of God is unshakable. When your life is built on it, you stand on solid rock, not shifting sand.

THE COST OF SURRENDER

You were designed to worship Him first. That is the architecture of your soul. Anything else placed in that position—career, relationships, money, health—will eventually collapse under the weight of your expectations. Only the Kingdom of God is unshakable. When your life is built on it, you stand on solid rock, not shifting sand.

Putting God first requires complete trust and full surrender. Our flesh resists this, even though our spirit longs for it. We say, *"Lord, be first,"* but wake up the next morning living as though we are still the masters of our own lives.

Most of us truly want to put God first. But we want to pleasure ourselves deeply—and the older we get, the harder it becomes. Years of self-rule train us to sit comfortably on the throne.

We crave safety, approval, acceptance, pleasure, and prosperity—the illusion of control. These cravings quietly rise as rivals for our devotion. Even good things—family, success, reputation, ministry—can become competitors for God's place when they begin to dictate our choices, moods, and sense of worth.

When that happens, they reveal themselves for what they truly are: **idols.**

Jesus made this unmistakably clear: *"If anyone would come after Me, let him deny himself, take up his cross, and follow Me."*

That is not a "live your best life" verse. That is not a motivational slogan, to seek your dreams. That is a call to surrender and obedience. *To deny himself and die daily!*

It sounds like a death sentence to the old self—because it is.

Many of us were taught that choosing God would simply make life easier. But following Christ does not offer convenience; it offers transformation.

DYING TO SELF IN A SELF-CENTERED WORLD

To put God first means embracing self-sacrifice in a world that worships the self. We are surrounded by messages that say, *"Follow your heart. Chase your dreams. Do what makes you happy."* Day after day, we absorb subtle invitations to prioritize comfort over obedience.

We fear losing ourselves because we have built our identity around what we love, what we enjoy, and what we control. Fear whispers that if we trust God fully, we will be disappointed. So we hedge our bets, holding back parts of our minds, hearts, and habits—keeping a quiet plan B.

Divided trust breeds spiritual misery.

Faithfulness is not a one-time vow; it is a daily battle. Every morning we must rise and say, *"Lord, sit on the throne of my life."* And then say it again tomorrow. And again the day after that.

We must ask God to tear down every idol—to crush every rival. Surrendering every thought, decision, relationship, and ambition will cost you—but it will also free you. Only God deserves first place. And only God can bear its weight.

If you feel a war raging inside you, do not be discouraged. It means your heart is alive. It means the Spirit is still stirring. It means you have not given up—only begun to give in.

This is what dying to self feels like.

IDENTIFYING RIVAL GODS

God cannot truly be God in your life until He is first. If we are not intentional, idols disguised as blessings will slip quietly into our hearts and demand loyalty.

Take money, for example. Money itself is not evil, yet how quickly it tries to crown itself as savior. We believe more money will bring peace, security, and favor. But Jesus warned plainly: *You cannot serve both God and money.* A master cannot share ownership of your heart.

Approval is another rival god. We were created for community, yet the desire to be liked and praised can become a prison. When fear of disappointing people outweighs fear of disappointing God, approval has taken His place.

Pleasure, too, can become a god. Pleasure is a gift when rightly ordered, but when pursued endlessly it devours peace and leaves emptiness in its wake.

Family can rival God's throne. Family is a blessing, but it makes a terrible god. It cannot save you, restore you, or carry your worship.

Fear may be the cruelest false god of all. Fear reshapes your life without ever rewarding you. When fear dictates your decisions, limits your obedience, and defines your calling—it has become your god.

REORDERING YOUR LIFE

You cannot serve two masters. Rival gods promise peace but deliver slavery. God's command—*"You shall have no other gods before Me"*—is not a threat. It is a rescue plan.

Putting God first requires reordering your life through daily, practical obedience.

Reorder your time.

Give God the first moments of your day—before your phone, before distractions. Even fifteen intentional minutes of Scripture, prayer, or worship can reshape the next twenty-four hours.

Reorder your money.

Where your treasure is, there your heart will be also. Generosity must be intentional. God cannot be first if He is absent from your finances.

Reorder your ambitions.

Surrender your goals to God's lordship. Ask not only, *"Is this good for me?"* but *"Does this honor God's kingdom?"*

Reorder your ambitions.

Surrender your goals to God's lordship. Ask not only, *"Is this good for me?"* but *"Does this honor God's kingdom?"*

LIVING WITH GOD FIRST

This is not sustained through one dramatic moment. It is built through hundreds of small, daily acts of surrender. God does not promise happiness—He promises salvation, redemption, and transformation.

To die daily requires constant realignment. Guard the throne of your heart. The world will always compete for first place.

But with the help of the Holy Spirit, you can walk in the power, freedom, and joy of a life where **God is truly first.**

CHAPTER 14
WHOLE BEFORE THE UNION THE SPIRITUAL GROWTH OF AN INDIVIDUAL

Personal Surrender Before Shared Promise
Union without division — this is where it all begins

Before there is ever true unity in marriage, there must first be ownership within the individual. A union without division is not built by two people trying to fix each other—it is built by two people fully committing to their own spiritual growth with each other before God.

No worries, if you are already married and believe that you are not whole there is still hope. Let's go.. Marriage does not remove personal responsibility. Marriage reveals it.

Too many people enter marriage believing union means transfer—transfer of happiness, transfer of stability, transfer of healing, transfer of things, transfer of purpose. But God's design is not transferred. God's design is alignment. Each person must first take ownership of their own spiritual condition, their own obedience, their own healing, and their own relationship with God.

You do not grow spiritually because you are married. You grow spiritually because you decide to submit in your marriage.

A marriage union does not replace growth—it demands it.

Spiritual Ownership Is the Foundation of a Godly Union. So this means each one needs to Put God First. It means I take full responsibility for my obedience.

So again, before I can fully belong to another in covenant, I must first fully belong to God in submission.

Yes, each one must pick up and carry their own cross. Okay, now we got it. Let's get moving forward.

This all starts with surrender — Because You Cannot Build a God-Centered Marriage with a Self-Centered Life

Many godly marriages quietly fracture because one or both spouses refuse to let go of their old identity. They want covenant benefits without covenant transformation.

But the covenant demands to die to yourself daily. A covenant life demands a renewal of the mind. A covenant life demands a discipline of the soul, surrender to the Holy Spirit and submission of the flesh. This is a life chosen for obedience over comfort. I know this is not what you were told or what you may have been taught. But God will not pour the weight of marriage on someone who refuses to grow beneath it. Growth prepares you for the weight of responsibility called "union."

The Marriage exposes immaturity, magnifies identity issues, and reveals spiritual gaps. When those concerns are not owned, they become a marriage of division.

The greatest protection a husband can give his marriage is not provision—it is obedience. The greatest contribution a wife can give her marriage is not respect —it is obedience. Submission and obedience to God are intertwined yet distinct. Spiritual growth and complete surrender is how you protect the union.

The evidence to see in a growing individual is one who prays instead of reacts, listens instead of defends, repents instead of blame, serves instead of demands, and most of all endures instead of escapes.

Spiritual ownership is what allows two people to say: "I will not use your weakness as an excuse for my disobedience."

Devotional Reflection

Before blaming your spouse for what is missing in the marriage, ask:

- What part of my own growth have I neglected?
- Where have I resisted God's correction?
- Where have I chosen comfort over obedience?
- Where have I protected myself instead of surrendering to God?

Spiritual growth is not loud—it is usually quiet and consistent. It is daily surrender in unseen places. It is obedience when no one is watching. And that quiet faithfulness becomes the loudest protection over a marriage.

Marriage is shared—but growth is personal.

The Power of Words and the Indwelling of the Holy Spirit

Our spiritual growth begins when we invite the Holy Spirit into our lives. Yet this invitation is not merely spoken once—it is continuously extended through the condition of our hearts and the words we choose to speak. Our words can welcome the Holy Spirit, or, when our hearts and minds are filled with fear or doubt, they can hinder His work within us. Scripture is clear: what we speak shapes our environment, our relationships, and even our future.

Every word we speak carries power—the power of life and death, to build up or tear down, to bless or to curse. The words we use daily help create the atmosphere in which we live. Because of this, we must be mindful that our words are not neutral; they are spiritual forces. They can draw the Holy Spirit near or push Him at a distance. When we speak words of kindness, peace, love, and gratitude, we create an environment where the Holy Spirit is welcome to dwell. But words rooted in anger, frustration, anxiety, and fear can block His presence. The Holy Spirit is drawn to peace, hope, trust, and surrender—not to doubt, fear, or discord.

In this way, our words either become an invitation or a barrier to God's presence. They reveal what is truly inside of us. So how do we create a life that invites the Holy Spirit in? It begins by aligning our hearts and minds with God's will. We must make a conscious decision to speak words that reflect God's truth and His love—words that agree with His promises rather than our fears. When we do this, we create an atmosphere where God can move freely in our lives.

Begin declaring peace, love, joy, and compassion over your life and your circumstances. Return to Scripture and allow God's Word to shape how you speak—especially when confronting fear, anxiety, frustration, or anger. You must intentionally make space for the Holy Spirit. Invite Him in through the words you speak and through daily practice. Over time, you will begin to notice a shift in your atmosphere. The Holy Spirit loves to dwell where He is welcomed.

This is not a one-time action; it is a daily discipline. Scripture consistently teaches that our words carry spiritual weight. They are never neutral. They either bring life or invite destruction into our situations.

Consider the words we speak to our families and loved ones. When we speak with kindness and encouragement, we build trust and peace. But when we speak harshly, in anger or frustration, we create an atmosphere of fear, tension, and division. Even in prayer, the posture of our words matters—words spoken in peace and love open the door for the Holy Spirit to dwell. Conversely, malicious gossip damages relationships, breeds anxiety, and can lead to isolation. The Holy Spirit responds to words that align with God's truth and His will.

Jesus sent the Holy Spirit so that God's presence would dwell within us. Understanding this truth changes everything. Rather than chasing emotional highs or fleeting spiritual moments, believers can step into the reality that God is always present—always speaking, always listening, and always ready to lead. So why do so many struggle to experience this awareness? Why does it seem difficult to maintain a sense of God's presence?

The answer is not found in striving harder or doing more. It is found in learning how to walk with the Holy Spirit. God's presence is not a place we visit; it is a place we are meant to dwell. The Holy Spirit does not come and go—He remains. The issue is not His absence, but our inability to recognize His presence. Distractions, fear, and doubt often cloud our sensitivity to His voice. The noise of life drowns out the gentle whisper of God's Spirit.

Instead of abiding, many find themselves reaching, stretching, and striving—believing they must earn what has already been freely given. The Holy Spirit is not a force or a fleeting experience. He is a person. He desires a relationship, not ritual. He longs to lead, but He will not force His way into our lives. He requires fellowship—a continual, surrendered walk with God.

The Holy Spirit is not reserved for the spiritually elite, nor for those who have reached a certain level of perfection or ministry. He is given to every believer. However, walking with Him requires a shift in perspective—a willingness to let go of old patterns of thinking, speaking, and acting. It requires openness, surrender, and trust.

This is not about religious performance or chasing mystical experiences. It is about cultivating a practical, daily relationship with God through His Spirit—a relationship where His voice becomes clearer, His guidance more recognizable, and His presence something we rest in rather than strive for. A relationship where prayer becomes an ongoing conversation, worship becomes a way of life, and surrender is no longer an event but a posture of the heart.

When a man takes responsibility for his wife, and a wife walks in accountability to her husband—both having placed God first and has invited the Holy Spirit into their lives daily—this is what emerges: a husband and wife like this…

CHAPTER 15
MY HUSBAND

The one who mirrors Christ relationship with the Church

Having a husband who embodies such rare and admirable qualities of provision, cultivation, selflessness, and understanding is a profound blessing. He stands apart as a man whose character, love, and devotion make him truly incomparable. His presence creates a sanctuary of support and understanding, nurturing a love that grows deeper with time. This kind of husband doesn't just fulfill the role of a partner; with understanding he becomes a trusted friend, a confidant, and a compassionate leader. His love is not superficial; it's deeply rooted, inspiring a sense of peace, joy, and fulfillment. Expressing appreciation for a husband like this involves reflecting on the remarkable qualities that make him so irreplaceable.

Understanding and Deep Connection

One of the most profound qualities of this type of husband is his ability to connect deeply with his spouse. He listens to his wife not just to respond or find a solution but to truly understand how she feels. This genuine interest in her thoughts and emotions shows her that he values her perspective and wants to connect with her on an emotional and intellectual level. He knows her well, often understanding her needs and feelings even before she fully understands them herself.

This husband creates a space of security where his wife feels seen and heard. He doesn't brush aside her feelings or jump to conclusions but instead takes the time to listen attentively, encouraging her to express herself without fear of judgment. This deep-rooted connection becomes the foundation of their relationship, making her feel loved and valued in ways words can barely describe. In this way, he becomes not just a husband but an irreplaceable presence, someone she cannot imagine life without.

An Empathetic Listener Who Values Her Perspective

Listening is an art that this husband has mastered. When his wife speaks, he listens with empathy and patience. He isn't focused solely on finding a solution; instead, he prioritizes understanding her emotions and thoughts and tries to connect with the story she gives him. This kind of listening is rare and transformative—it creates an environment of trust and emotional intimacy that strengthens their bond and gives her the friend she yearns for.

He understands that sometimes his wife simply needs to be heard and that she may not need a solution every time. By being there to listen, he helps her process her thoughts and feelings. This empathetic approach helps her feel deeply supported, making her willing and confident in sharing her thoughts and emotions with him.

Patience and Conflict Avoidance

Another remarkable quality of this husband is his ability to handle conflict with patience and calmness. Even when his wife may be experiencing difficult emotions or acting unreasonably, he doesn't react impulsively or get drawn into unnecessary arguments. Instead, he maintains his composure, knowing that understanding and calmness are far more effective than confrontation and reacting.

His approach to conflict prevents misunderstandings and distances from growing between them. His gentle handling of situations that could otherwise escalate shows his commitment to preserving harmony and love in their relationship. By approaching challenges with patience and empathy, he shows his wife that she is more important to him than any momentary disagreement. This patience is a sign of his emotional maturity and deep commitment to their relationship, making her feel secure and loved, even during challenging times.

A True Friend and Confidant

Beyond being a husband, he is also a trusted friend—a friend she can confide in without fear of being judged or misunderstood. He offers a safe space where she can express her worries, dreams, and insecurities. His support during difficult times reassures her that she is never alone, no matter what life brings. Knowing she has someone who listens without judgment, someone who genuinely cares about her experiences, fosters a trust that builds the bedrock of their relationship.

This friendship aspect of their relationship strengthens their bond even further. He's not just a partner in name but someone who genuinely cares about her well-being, someone who is willing to listen and offer comfort. She knows she can lean on him, and this sense of security builds a profound connection that goes beyond romance. In him, she finds a friend who supports her growth, encourages her dreams, and provides unwavering loyalty.

Non-Judgmental and Compassionate in Emotional Moments

This husband knows that emotions are complex, and he doesn't judge his wife for how she feels. Instead, he approaches her emotions with compassion and understanding, recognizing that she needs to emote and they are a natural part of her experience. When she is emotional, he takes the time to listen, ask gentle questions, and help her feel grounded and understood. This thoughtful approach strengthens their connection, as she feels safe to share her inner world without fear of being dismissed or criticized.

He doesn't react defensively or jump to conclusions. Instead, he takes the time to ask the necessary questions, showing her that he is willing to understand her deeply and completely. This level of compassion makes her feel valued and understood, reinforcing the trust that forms the foundation of their marriage. His ability to provide this safe emotional space is a testament to his maturity, empathy, and dedication to their relationship.

A Willingness to Please and Comfort

One of the things that makes this husband so special is his eagerness to please and comfort his wife. He puts her needs above his own, making her feel cherished and cared for. His selflessness reflects his love and commitment, as he constantly seeks ways to make her feel happy and supported. This devotion is not just about grand gestures but about the small, everyday acts that show his love and dedication.

His willingness to prioritize her well-being makes her feel the most important person to him and loved in a profound way. She knows that she is not only important to him but that he genuinely desires to please her. This selfless love fosters an atmosphere of appreciation and mutual respect, creating a foundation of trust and joy in their relationship.

Leading with Patience, Kindness, and Confidence

This husband's leadership is defined by patience, kindness, and confidence. He doesn't impose his will but leads with a calm assurance that inspires trust and respect. His kindness and patience create an atmosphere where his wife feels comfortable to follow his lead, knowing that his intentions and actions are rooted in love and consideration for her well-being. His leadership is not about control but about guiding their relationship and family with a steady hand and a loving heart. I call it steady love.

His confidence is not overbearing but rather an assurance that he will always act in their best interest. This gentle strength gives his wife a sense of security and admiration, making her eager to support and follow him. His leadership encourages her to grow and thrive, as he creates an environment where she feels safe, loved, and supported.

Encouragement and Uplifting Support

One of the most inspiring qualities of this husband is his ability to encourage his wife. He speaks life into her, constantly supporting her dreams, aspirations, and personal growth. He sees her beautiy as a person despite any flaws or shortcoming as his gift and inspires her to become her best self. His words and actions reflect a deep belief in her, which gives her the confidence to pursue becoming a better her and for her environment.

He provides encouragement not only in words but also through actions, showing her that he is genuinely invested in her happiness and success. His support helps her feel confident and empowered, knowing she has a partner who believes in her fully. This kind of encouragement strengthens her sense of self-worth and makes her feel deeply loved and appreciated.

Correcting with Love and Compassion

This husband doesn't shy away from guiding his wife when he feels it is necessary, but he does so with compassion and love. His correction is not harsh or punitive; it is motivated by a desire to help her grow and improve. He understands that love includes helping each other become better people, and his gentle correction shows her that he genuinely cares about her well-being and personal growth.

When he offers guidance, he does so in a way that makes her feel influenced to do so and supported rather than criticized. His approach to correction strengthens their bond, as she knows he is looking out for her with love and respect. His compassion in these moments deepens her love for him, as she feels safe to grow and learn in his presence.

A Profound Sense of Gratitude and Love

With a husband like this, gratitude becomes a natural response. Every day, his wife feels thankful for his presence, his love, and his dedication. She loves him not only for who he is but also for the way he makes her feel—understood, valued, and supported. Her love for him is deeply rooted in the way he treats her, a love that grows with each act of kindness, patience, and understanding.

His unique combination of compassion, understanding, and selflessness makes her feel deeply loved, respected, priceless. She admires him not only for his qualities but for the way he lives those qualities every day, creating a relationship that is rooted in love, trust, and mutual respect. Her love for him is a reflection of his love for her, a love that is built on a foundation of genuine care and unwavering support.

CHAPTER 16
MY WIFE

A good cooperative affectionate nurturing helper

Having a wife who is rooted in her femininity makes her incomparable to others is truly a rare and cherished gift. Such a woman embodies a depth of understanding, compassion, and submission that creates a foundation of strength and harmony in a relationship. Breathtaking. This kind of wife isn't only defined by her femininity but also by her submission and surrender—her genuine love, gratitude, and respect for her husband and her unwavering commitment to nurturing a fulfilling, stable, and peaceful home — *rare*. A wife like this stands apart because her approach to life and marriage transcends everyday challenges, allowing her to provide not only cooperation but strength in a deeply supportive, balanced relationship.

A Deep and Respectful Communication Style

One of the most remarkable qualities of a wife like this is her exceptional understanding of communication. She knows that healthy communication isn't about excessive words or unpacking every detail; rather, it's about understanding her husband's needs and his nature and fostering a meaningful dialogue that respects those needs. When a problem arises, she approaches it with directness and a solution-focused mindset, not bogging down in emotional weight or lengthy explanations. When she needs to vent and be heard, she approaches it with clarity and directs her husband to be her soundboard and no need for resolution. She doesn't expect him to guest or figure it out, or worse she doesn't demand that he should know her and all her emotions by now! She recognizes that effective communication is based on the understanding of who they are, individual, especially knowing the nature of her husband; always leading with clarity, understanding, and patience.

This wife doesn't need her husband to recount every moment of his day; she understands that sometimes, less is more. She's aware that men often process stress differently and doesn't impose her desires and communication style on him. When he's stressed or carrying the weight of the day's demands, she is a calming presence, instinctively knowing when to keep conversations brief, focusing only on essential points without diving into lengthy discussions. Her ability to communicate with empathy and wisdom enables her husband to feel supported and understood without feeling overwhelmed, helping maintain a peaceful and open atmosphere in the relationship.

Furthermore, she understands and respects her husband's need for silence during difficult times. She doesn't pressure him to communicate when he's not ready, understanding that sometimes silence allows for internal processing and healing. This understanding creates an environment where her husband feels free to express himself when he's ready, without feeling rushed or obligated. Such an approach fosters genuine respect and helps preserve harmony within the home.

Embracing Femininity and Kindness

Her femininity is another aspect that sets this wife apart. She understands the power of kindness, softness, and approachability, which enhances the bond with her husband is very necessary. Instead of creating tension or challenging his role, she embraces her unique qualities, allowing her natural gentleness and warmth to attract him to her rather than push him away and encourage a harmonious relationship.

This wife doesn't pressure her husband to intuitively understand all her needs or desires. Instead, she communicates openly, making her feelings known in a respectful and clear way that strengthens their connection. She doesn't expect her husband to "just know" what she's thinking or feeling; rather, she willingly shares her thoughts and shares her feelings in a way that is constructive and supportive, avoiding frustration and miscommunication. This openness and grace encourage her husband to be attentive, and it strengthens his desire to care for her fully and thoughtfully. Giving him many ways and reasons to appreciate her presence.

A Woman of Faith and Stewardship

Rooted in her faith, this wife does not seek validation or happiness through material possessions. She is neither frivolous with her spending nor fixated on superficial desires. Instead, she finds contentment in her relationship with God, and this inner peace influences her outlook on finances and resources. She's resourceful with little and wise with much, understanding that true abundance is measured by the love and stability within her family rather than by material wealth.

Her faith gives her a clear sense of purpose and provides her with the strength to navigate life's challenges with resilience and grace. By managing resources responsibly, she contributes to a household that is both financially stable and spiritually grounded, enhancing the family's overall sense of security. This attitude towards wealth and resources, combined with her faith-centered approach, creates a solid foundation that reflects her commitment to being a blessing to her family. She is like a priceless gem.

Contributing Without Controlling

In her marriage, she seeks to contribute rather than control. She supports her husband's leadership and vision, trusting his guidance while also sharing her wisdom and insights in a way that adds value without undermining his role. Her contributions are made with humility and respect, aiming to build up rather than assert dominance or control. She trusts in his leadership even when times are challenging and confident enough to lean back in faith that his knowledge and provision is sufficient.

This attitude of contribution and submission allows her husband to grow into his role with confidence and assurance. He feels supported rather than pressured, knowing that his wife values and respects his leadership. Her willingness to contribute in this way strengthens their relationship, creating a balanced dynamic where both feel valued and appreciated.

A Balanced Approach to Parenting

As a mother, she is committed to the growth and discipline of her children, even when it challenges her emotionally. She believes in the importance of discipline and structure, recognizing that these values are essential for raising responsible and resilient children. She is willing to teach the hard lessons of life, even when they conflict with her natural inclination to protect and shield her children from discomfort. By instilling discipline and a strong sense of order, she prepares her children to face the world with strength and integrity.

This balance between nurture and discipline reflects her maturity and selflessness as a parent. She does not allow her emotions to cloud her judgment or prevent her from doing what is best for her children in the long run. Her approach to parenting reinforces her children's sense of stability and helps them develop a clear understanding of right and wrong, empowering them to grow into well-rounded, morally grounded individuals.

Expressing Appreciation and Fostering Connection

This wife appreciates her husband deeply and shows it daily through both words and actions. She expresses gratitude not only through affectionate gestures but also through the respect and care she shows in their daily interactions. Her appreciation is genuine, reflecting a deep love and admiration that inspires her husband to continue providing and caring for her with all his heart.

Her respect for her husband's role and her genuine appreciation for his efforts make him feel valued and needed. This mutual respect fosters an atmosphere of love and trust, where both partners feel secure and motivated to continue building a meaningful life together. Her ability to express appreciation openly and consistently strengthens their bond, enhancing the overall quality of their relationship.

Inspiring Through Respect and Submission

One of the most captivating qualities of this wife is her respect and willingness to submit to her husband's leadership. Her approach to submission isn't about weakness but about trust and admiration. She honors his role as a provider and leader, encouraging him to grow and thrive. Her respect makes her incredibly attractive in her husband's eyes; he gravitates to her, and he's drawn to her in ways that words alone cannot describe.

Her respectful submission is a powerful source of motivation, inspiring him to be the best man he can be. Her admiration and support encourage him to take on his responsibilities with integrity and dedication, knowing that he has her unwavering support. This cycle of mutual respect and admiration creates a fulfilling relationship where both partners feel valued and motivated to serve each other wholeheartedly.

Encouraging Excellence in Life and Faith

In her presence, her husband feels encouraged to be his best self. Her love and respect are transformative, motivating him to pursue excellence in his work, character, and spiritual life. She stands by him, not only as a loving wife but as a true partner who wants the best for him in every aspect of life. Her encouragement is pure and genuine, never demanding or conditional, which allows him to grow freely and joyfully.

Her influence is profound; she inspires him to be a better man not through demands but through the gentle, soft encouragement of her presence, love, and respect. Her faith in him and her ability to see his goodness create a space where he feels both challenged and supported, striving to reach his highest potential out of love and respect for her.

Final Reflections: A Love Beyond Compare

In every sense, this wife is incomparable. Her love, faithfulness, and dedication go beyond what is often seen or expected. She is more than a companion; she is a source of strength, peace, and inspiration. Her respect, her gentle nature, her wisdom, and her faith create an atmosphere of love and stability that makes her husband's life richer and more meaningful.

Having such a wife is a profound blessing—a relationship that transcends the ordinary, providing a wellspring of joy, purpose, and spiritual growth. Her commitment, her virtue, and her love are qualities that make her truly irreplaceable. This is a wife who not only fulfills the role of a partner but elevates it into something holy and deeply cherished. This is a wife who submits herself to her husband as she does to the Lord. And when this happens without self protection it falls into a deep life of appreciation of one another—a testament to what it means to share a life guided by love and rooted in faith. A union designed for an intimate life and built without division.

CHAPTER 17
SHARING THE SIX AREAS OF INTIMACY
The Six Areas of Intimacy: A godly Way

1. Showing Appreciation

Expressing appreciation for your significant other is a fundamental and powerful way to strengthen the bond between you and your partner. Building intimacy in a relationship involves more than grand gestures or occasional acts of doing nice things; it hinges on daily efforts that nurture connection and closeness. One of the most important and crucial ways of building intimacy is showing genuine appreciation with your words. When you express gratitude and appreciation regularly, it reinforces trust, understanding, and affection. Here's why and how verbal appreciation plays a transformative role in deepening intimacy:

Just like Our Lord and Savior Jesus Christ as He spoke giving comfort, peace, and joy to those who heard them.

The Power of Words in a Relationship

Words are more than just communication tools; they are expressions of our inner thoughts and feelings. In a relationship, positive and affirming words act as connectors that bind partners emotionally. Keeping your words is more important than speaking them without a true foundation. By expressing appreciation to your significant other daily, you create a consistent reminder of their value in your life. This reassurance can make them feel cherished and seen, which strengthens emotional security and nurtures intimacy.

When you tell your partner, "I'm so grateful for you," or "I feel blessed to have you in my life," it affirms your recognition of their efforts and presence. These expressions show that you don't take their love and contributions for granted. The act of verbal appreciation is not just a formality—it is an acknowledgment of the shared journey and the unique role your partner plays in your life.

Daily Words of Appreciation and Gratitude

Incorporating words of gratitude into your daily routine is one of the simplest yet most impactful ways to maintain personal and relational intimacy. Each day, make it a point to express your love and appreciation for your partner. It could be as simple as saying, "Thank you for always being here for me," or "I really admire how thoughtful you are." Such statements might seem small, but they carry profound meaning. They remind your partner that their presence and actions do not go unnoticed.

Recognizing the quiet, often overlooked contributions your partner makes can be particularly powerful. Whether it's their willingness to listen to you after a long day, taking care of small tasks, or supporting you in subtle ways, expressing your awareness of these gestures can mean a lot. For instance, telling your partner,

"I noticed how you made sure everything was ready before our guests arrived—I really appreciate your attention to detail," shows that you see and value their care and effort.

Expressing Love Mindfully

It's crucial to express your appreciation mindfully, ensuring that your words reflect genuine respect and gratitude. This involves being cautious and careful with what you say, recognizing that your words carry weight on how you say them. When you are mindful of how you express yourself, it communicates to your partner that you not only value them but also respect the trust and vulnerability that exist between you.

Using uplifting words can turn an ordinary moment into an opportunity to strengthen your connection. Encouraging your partner when they face challenges or simply reminding them of their strengths can deepen the intimacy between you. For example, "I am always amazed by how resilient you are; it inspires me every day," or "You are so talented, and I believe in you" are ways to use words to build confidence and convey appreciation.

Acts of Kindness and Respect

While words are powerful, pairing them with acts of kindness and respect enhances their effect. Demonstrating appreciation through small acts, such as bringing your partner their favorite treat, doing chores they usually handle, or planning a surprise that aligns with their interests, can be an extension of your verbal appreciation. It shows that you pay attention to their likes and needs and are willing to put effort into making them feel loved.

Doing things that lighten your partner's load—whether it's taking on an extra errand or handling a household task—can be an act of service that communicates appreciation. It not only helps relieve some of their daily pressures but also sends the message that their well-being matters to you. This kind of thoughtfulness reinforces a sense of partnership and mutual support, which are critical components of intimacy.

Never Taking Your Partner for Granted

Perhaps the most significant way to show appreciation is by not taking your partner for granted. Consistently expressing your gratitude and being present in your relationship are tangible ways to show that you cherish your significant other. Simple acts, such as saying "thank you" for giving a genuine smile, may seem minor, but when done regularly, they cultivate an environment of positivity and warmth.

Seizing moments to express thankfulness, whether through words, smiles, or loving gestures, fosters an atmosphere where intimacy can flourish. It affirms to your partner that they are valued not just for what they do but for who they are. This daily reinforcement of appreciation builds a solid foundation for enduring intimacy and love.

Appreciating your significant other through words, paired with acts of kindness and respect, plays a crucial role in maintaining and deepening intimacy. Deep intimacy is built outside of the bedroom that makes the inside of the bedroom, WOW! Mindful and regular expressions of gratitude create a safe space where love, trust, and affection can grow. Making the conscious choice to honor and uplift your partner strengthens your connection and ensures that your bond remains strong and vibrant.

2. Constant Open Vulnerable Communication

Vulnerability is one of the most powerful yet often overlooked aspects of building deep intimacy in a relationship. It is the act of exposing oneself emotionally, revealing true thoughts, feelings, fears, and desires. This emotional openness is not a weakness but a strength that can transform the foundation of a relationship, creating a space for genuine connection and trust. The importance of vulnerability in a relationship cannot be understated; it's a bridge that connects two people in a meaningful and profound way.

The Power of Vulnerability and Acceptance

Being vulnerable with your partner is a powerful way to increase intimacy because it fosters an environment of honesty and acceptance. When both partners are willing to be open and expose their inner selves, it allows for a deeper understanding and acceptance of one another. Vulnerability can come in many forms, from admitting fears and insecurities to sharing dreams and aspirations. Each time partners share these deeper aspects of themselves, they strengthen their emotional connection.

However, in order to reach this level of intimacy, one must first accept themselves for who they are. Self-acceptance lays the groundwork for being able to share openly with another person. Without accepting your flaws, strengths, and everything in between, it's difficult to let someone else fully into your world. When you embrace who you are, vulnerability becomes less about risking rejection and more about inviting your partner into your true self. This self-acceptance can lead to increased emotional safety in the relationship, where both partners feel free to be authentic.

The Benefits of Emotional Exposure

The act of being emotionally exposed may come with the fear of uncertainty, but it holds the potential for deep rewards. The vulnerability of revealing feelings, whether it's expressing love, admitting mistakes, or confronting fears, can open the door to a connection that's more genuine and loving. This openness allows partners to understand each other on a level that surpasses surface interactions. It communicates that each person trusts the other enough to share their most guarded thoughts and emotions.

The benefits of such emotional exposure are numerous. It allows for a relationship in which both partners feel seen and valued. By being vulnerable, you invite your partner to be vulnerable too, creating a reciprocal bond that's hard to break. This type of open communication can bring newfound closeness and empathy, making the relationship not just a partnership but a haven where both individuals can grow.

Boosting Confidence and Facing Challenges Together

When two people share honest and open communication consistently, it boosts confidence in their intimate interactions. Knowing that your partner is open to hearing and understanding your feelings creates a sense of safety and security. This, in turn, makes it easier to express love and affection, explore desires, and handle conflicts more constructively. Confidence in intimacy is not just about physical closeness; it's about feeling safe to be emotionally open without judgment.

Moreover, vulnerability equips partners to face life's difficulties more effectively. When a couple builds a foundation of open communication, they learn to support each other through challenges and hardships. This mutual support strengthens their bond and helps them face uncertainties with a united front. Additionally, this type of emotional sharing can improve self-acceptance as partners witness firsthand that they are loved and valued despite their imperfections.

Deepening Connection and Opening Doors

Relationships that prioritize vulnerability open doors that often remain closed in typical relationships. It allows for conversations and experiences that others may never reach. This closeness comes from a willingness to share without fear of judgment or rejection, creating a relationship where even the most sensitive topics can be discussed freely. The result is a profound connection that feels unexplainable yet fulfilling and rare.

This kind of relationship is built on essential pillars such as honesty, openness, and forgiveness. Honesty encourages transparency and trust, allowing both partners to show up as their true selves. Openness fosters an environment where thoughts and emotions can be shared without reservation. Forgiveness is crucial because mistakes and misunderstandings are inevitable, but how partners respond to them will determine whether they build or break intimacy. Patience ties all these together, as vulnerability is not always easy and requires time and practice to fully integrate into a relationship.

Embracing Love and Self-Love

An intimacy that is rooted in love also embraces self-love. When partners are willing to be vulnerable, they show that they accept not only their partner's imperfections but their own. This acceptance makes it easier to let go of shame and guilt. Instead of holding onto mistakes or past hurts, they can acknowledge and release them, knowing that their relationship is a safe space for growth and healing.

Ultimately, the deepest connections are formed when both partners create an environment where vulnerability is welcomed and respected. This kind of intimacy cannot thrive without honesty, openness, forgiveness, and patience. In this space, partners are not just in a relationship but are true allies who support each other's growth, embrace flaws, and cherish the trust that binds them. It's through this continuous and courageous vulnerability that a relationship transcends ordinary love, becoming something profound and enduring.

3. Private Relationship

Maintaining privacy in a relationship is crucial for building and nurturing an intimate bond. When a relationship is kept private, it creates a safe and sacred space where partners can be vulnerable without fear of judgment or interference. This safe space allows them to share their deepest thoughts, fears, and desires, fostering trust and emotional security. When partners know that what they share stays between them, it encourages honesty and openness, which are essential for true intimacy.

Preserving privacy also enhances the opportunity for quality time, which is vital for deepening a connection. Without the distractions of outside influences or the need to present a curated version of the relationship, couples can focus on each other and engage in meaningful interactions. This undivided attention strengthens the emotional bond and makes it easier to navigate challenges together. In private moments, partners can be themselves, free from the pressure to meet social expectations or showcase their relationship.

Privacy in a relationship also allows couples to prioritize their own needs and lifestyle without external pressures. When a relationship is exposed to the opinions of friends, family, or social media, it can lead to unrealistic expectations and comparisons that may strain the partnership. Keeping certain aspects of the relationship private ensures that decisions are made based on what is best for the couple, rather than external validation or approval. This fosters a stronger, more unified bond and allows the relationship to grow on its own terms, rooted in genuine love and understanding.

4. Physical Intimacy

Physical intimacy is an essential element of a healthy, thriving relationship. It encompasses more than just sexual interactions; it includes all forms of physical touch, such as holding hands, hugging, kissing, and cuddling. These expressions of closeness foster a deep emotional bond and create a desire to be in each other's presence. The importance of physical intimacy lies in its ability to build trust, increase affection, and strengthen the overall connection between partners.

Physical touch acts as a powerful form of nonverbal communication. When partners engage in physical intimacy, it conveys care, love, and support without words. Simple acts such as a warm embrace or a reassuring touch on the arm can communicate comfort, safety, and solidarity. These gestures help build a sense of security and belonging, making both partners feel valued and cherished. This feeling of closeness becomes a foundation that supports emotional intimacy, creating a deeper attachment and a greater desire to spend time together.

As a relationship grows, it's important for couples to prioritize and continue increasing physical touch. Just as regular communication and quality time are necessary to maintain a strong relationship, so too is maintaining consistent physical contact. Over time, the stresses of life, work, or family responsibilities can sometimes lead partners to deprioritize physical affection. However, keeping physical intimacy alive requires conscious effort and should be seen as an ongoing commitment. Regular physical touch helps sustain the initial spark of the relationship and strengthens the bond, reinforcing the emotional connection.

The significance of maintaining healthy physical intimacy cannot be overstated. When physical affection is lacking, it often leads to feelings of neglect, loneliness, and emotional disconnection. Partners may begin to feel undervalued or isolated when touch is absent, creating a sense of distance. This distance can eventually erode communication, causing misunderstandings or making partners reluctant to share their feelings and thoughts openly. Without physical intimacy, the sense of closeness that once brought joy and unity to the relationship starts to fade, leading to potential dissatisfaction or estrangement.

A lack of physical connection can also impact desires for one another. When touch becomes infrequent or absent, the desire for intimacy can wane. This can lead to a vicious cycle where emotional disconnection decreases physical affection, and the lack of physical affection further fuels emotional withdrawal. In such scenarios, couples may experience a breakdown in communication and a decrease in overall relationship satisfaction.

Physical touch plays a fundamental role in ensuring that intimacy is maintained. Without it, the relationship is at risk of becoming stagnant or emotionally distant. The connection that partners build through touch helps maintain their emotional well-being and strengthens the relationship's resilience during tough times. Holding hands, hugging, or simply being close to one another can create a calming and reassuring effect, making partners feel supported.

In summary, it is nearly impossible to build and maintain a truly intimate relationship without physical touch. Physical intimacy bridges the emotional and physical divide, ensuring that the relationship remains vibrant, fulfilling, and secure. To keep a relationship healthy, couples should make a concerted effort to maintain and increase physical touch as they grow together, reinforcing their emotional bond and sustaining their desire for one another.

What About SEX!

Marriage is a sacred union designed to intertwine two lives so deeply that they become one in mind, spirit, and body. This intimacy creates a bond so vulnerable, so codependent, and so full of servitude that it becomes a reflection of the deepest kind of love. Physical intimacy in marriage is not just an act of passion; it is an expression of unity, trust, and mutual devotion. When nurtured in the right context, it brings a joy that is unmatched, fostering a connection that elevates the marital bond to profound depths.

Sexual intimacy within marriage was created to be both joyous and fulfilling, a gift meant to be shared and enjoyed exclusively by husband and wife. This sacred connection is not just about physical pleasure but about expressing love and vulnerability in a way that strengthens the entire relationship. When both partners commit to shared principles, behaviors, and beliefs, and when their desire is to genuinely please and serve one another, their sexual experiences transcend the physical. Each encounter becomes a moment of profound closeness, elevating their relationship to levels of intimacy that are almost overwhelming in their intensity.

Okay, What About SEX!

No.., not like that. Let's talk about sex without really talking about sex. This is still a family book, Lol.

Okay, let's start with understanding the sexual satisfaction for women. In godly marriages sex is a vital aspect of a healthy relationship. For a man to truly love a woman, he must understand her desires, engage in meaningful conversations, and want to learn how to satisfy her sexually. Many may not believe it is important in a godly relationship but sex was designed for a godly relationship.

Today many marriages have high expectations around sex and romance. With many women they find a need to express themselves and their desire to be fulfilled in their relationship, as a must! To truly satisfy a woman sexually, a man must have a clear understanding of their own vulnerability, and how to communicate to discover the needs of their partner. A man must be willing to understand the female's body and how it connects emotionally. Many times a man must learn and understand her past. To please a woman sexually is all in understanding her intimately, honest communication, and much practice. This includes learning how to intrigue, arouse, and make an emotional impact on her thoughts and feelings. This means good deep conversations.

Most of what begins with meaningful conversations about her desires, boundaries, past experiences, and expectations. Ask her what pleases her and find out if she has had any bad experiences. If you are not as open and eager as her, try not to judge her and let go of any of your shortcomings. To dive deep in gilding this type of intimacy requires much communication. This will help build trust and emotional intimacy, which are prerequisites for female sexual connection. The more you communicate and build this bond it allows her to explore and express her desire. With healthy and honest communication It eliminates confusion and guesswork or conflicts. Most women want to converse about sex and want you to ask and share as much information as possible.

Trying to understand every woman is difficult and unique. Try not to group their emotional feelings and emotional experiences. Discover with meaningful conversation her own set of desires, preferences and experiences. To love her on a deeper level you should really like being around her, then discover what she likes, dislikes, and what excites her both physically and emotionally. Explore her inner desires. Explore if she enjoys spontaneity or a carefully planned experience. Understanding her sexual history can reveal what has worked for her in the past and what hasn't.

Women and men need an emotional bond to fully enjoy physical intimacy. Building trust and showing affection outside the bedroom will enhance her experience inside the bedroom. Being attentive and responsive to her feedback is crucial. Most important in this journey is being mindful of the words you use and more importantly how you use them. Pay attention to her body language, verbal cues, and expressions to understand what brings her pleasure when conversing.

Foreplay is often the gateway to a satisfying sexual experience for women and men. It helps build anticipation, arousal, and a deeper connection. For women foreplay starts with verbal banter. Compliment her, express your desires for her, and use sensual talk to set the mood. Physical foreplay starts with gentle caresses, kisses, and massages to awaken her senses. It is very important to take your time especially if it is your first time with her.

For those men that have less experience and confidence and find themselves already married, let her know where you are at, and you are willing to learn more how to satisfy her, with her patience. Ask many questions and learn as much about women and learn about your woman and her past experiences, share, share your experiences and learn hers.

In conclusion when it comes to sexual needs in a relationship, women often desire a deeper, more emotional experience that surpasses just the physical satisfaction. Approach intimacy with curiosity and enthusiasm and create a safe and pleasurable space. Spending a good amount of time with your partner is important to maximize her experience. Also, with most women constant check-ins with them and healthy banter conversing is always plus. Discovering the things to help her distress helps with the intimate times, and how much you desire her happiness. Every woman wants their man to desire them where they can barely go a day without wanting them physically, even in the times they don't want you to touch them. Lol.

Okay, now men. Understanding sexual satisfaction for men is a little more simple. Because most men can easily be satisfied by their physical and visual connection with sexual tension and attraction. This mostly depends on their perception and the acceptance that you want them as well. They also need a woman to be friendly and share their interest with you. Understanding his likes, dislikes, and what excites him is a plus for most men, not a demand. For some men it might be a requirement.

Most men, especially men over forty would prefer not to talk much about their past experiences and their intimate feelings regarding sex. Why, because they are men. No! This is because many men are very sensitive in this area. If you have any reservation of how and what you expect from your man, maybe you should be careful with this topic until your connection is strong. But if you do have any demands or must have with your man let him know. Most men won't know or figure this out on their own. This is the time to communicate all your desires. Don't expect your man to know because you've been together for years. Tell him. Just be aware of what type of man you are dealing with, an extra sexual or a conservative man, because many conservative men you may slowly push him away or he may start to become disinterested in you. Be careful sharing your open and wild experiences if it doesn't seem like he is interested in hearing about your wild side..

For men, foreplay starts with verbal banter, touching, and appreciation. Yes, feeling desired and accepted just like women are the highest contributor of fulfilling their sexual satisfaction. These acts also keep the foreplay active. We talk in genuine attraction and interest in being intimate with them. Many men relate your attraction and interest in them to their emotional satisfaction with their sexual experience. Men appreciate a partner who is responsive, expressive, and actively engages and initiates sex. Regular physical closeness helps maintain connection and fuels sexual desire for both. For men, freedom to express desire and their preferences without fear of shame or rejection helps build intimacy and will make him gravitate more to you. For many men a high level of respect also plays an important role in building intimacy and sexual connection. I believe consistent sexual connection often matters for both because both desire emotional and physical intimacy that is reciprocal and meaningful.

For the men who struggle with performance anxiety, fears of inadequacy, or discomfort in discussing sexual matters—patience, compassion, and desire. That's if you truly want that man. If you want this man, not just love him, but want him, educate yourself and practice mindful actions with your words. Remember healthy sexual relationships are about connection, not perfection.

Imagine growing this type of connection that requires both partners to be committed to serving one another in their sexual intimacy. This type of relationship is one built on mutual respect, selflessness, intentional communication, and desire. In such a bond, each person regularly seeks to understand and fulfill the other's desires, creating a space where vulnerability and pleasure are deeply connected and honored. They frequently ask thoughtful questions, exploring what brings joy and satisfaction to their partner. Questions like, "What makes you feel most desired?" or "How can I make you feel closer to me?" open doors to deeper connection and trust.

Both partners approach this process with delight and diligence, eager to learn about each other's needs and preferences. They make it a priority to communicate openly, sharing their emotions, physical desires, and even their fears, ensuring that neither feels neglected or misunderstood. By discussing the many factors that influence attraction—such as mood, environment, and emotional connection—they foster a deeper understanding of how to please and cherish one another. Remember you are not yours. For men women need for you to seed into her soul daily as much as you can. This means use your words to tell her how beautiful she looks in those jeans, dress and so on. Tell her you like it when she laughs like that and the way she scoots back into you when you're in bed together, like that. Tell her she's so beautiful inside and out. Tell her how attracted you are to her and even more so after all these years. For women, men need you to feed into him and nurture his mind—through his eyes and his belief that you are only his, nurture his body—through the nurturing of your hands, don't just cook for him, serve him every opportunity you can. This also means being attractive for him, looking like you want him to keep his eyes always planted on you. These things practice regularly adds to the intimacy rooted into a one sexual experience and the whole relationship.

These intentional efforts elevate their sexual intimacy to a higher level, strengthening their bond. They view this connection not just as a source of pleasure but as a vital aspect of their relationship, deepening their unity and commitment with each shared moment of passion. From the simplest ways they share pleasing looks at one another to the subtle ways their body language talks, to the force that draws them to touch one another always feeling accepted, appreciated, and belonging seems unmatchable.

However, this joy and fulfillment require balance. Marriage was designed to include God as an integral part of the relationship, ensuring that physical intimacy does not become unbalanced or overshadow the other aspects of the union. A focus on spiritual and emotional growth, alongside physical satisfaction, ensures that the relationship remains healthy and purposeful.

Marital intimacy should not just satisfy physical desires but create a deeper emotional and spiritual connection with each act. Couples are meant to experience the ultimate satisfaction of the flesh in a way that reflects their unity and devotion, building a bond that grows stronger with every encounter and aligns with the divine intention of marriage.

5. Solitude

I know we spoke about this, but let me reiterate because most people are just not aware. Again, solitude is a fundamental component that allows individuals and couples to deepen their bond, strengthen their resilience, and foster a space for emotional growth. **Solitude can be a powerful tool in fostering a healthy physical, emotional, spiritual and** fulfilling relationship. When individuals in a relationship dedicate time to themselves, they create opportunities for self-reflection and personal growth. Spending quality time alone allows each person to evaluate their feelings, interactions, and contributions within the relationship. Did I treat my wife well this week? Did I speak kindly to my husband this week? This introspection helps individuals identify personal shortcomings and areas for improvement, enhancing self-awareness and emotional intelligence. By recharging and addressing personal needs, individuals bring their best selves into the relationship.

In addition to personal solitude, spending time together as a couple in solitude, away from worldly distractions, strengthens intimacy as mentioned. This quiet, undisturbed time allows partners to deepen their bond, focus on each other's presence, and nurture their connection through personal attention and service. It fosters meaningful conversations, shared experiences, and a renewed appreciation for one another, which are vital for maintaining a strong relationship.

Honesty about the need for alone time is essential. When partners openly communicate their need for self-care, it builds trust and mutual understanding. This honesty ensures that taking personal space is not perceived as withdrawal but as a healthy practice that benefits the relationship. Respecting each other's individuality strengthens the connection by promoting emotional balance and reducing potential conflicts.

Regular intervals of time apart can also rekindle desire and curiosity within the relationship. Absence often makes the heart grow fonder, and the longing to reconnect can lead to renewed passion and excitement. Time apart allows each partner to miss the other, reigniting feelings of appreciation and desire.

Ultimately, balancing personal solitude, shared quiet time, and honest communication creates a harmonious relationship dynamic. It ensures that both individuals can thrive individually as a couple, fostering deeper connection and long-term fulfillment. However spending healthy time together has the most powerful impact and influences on any type of relationship.

6. Spending time together

One of the most powerful ways to build and maintain an intimate relationship is through spending quantity and quality time together. Among all the other areas of intimacy that contribute to a successful relationship—such as communication, trust, and respect, and all the other areas of intimacy—spending time together is arguably the most important. Feeling close and connected to your significant other often stems from shared experiences and consistent presence in each other's lives. Partners who prioritize spending time with one another create a foundation that supports emotional intimacy and long-lasting love.

Relationships thrive on shared moments. When partners make a conscious effort to spend time together, they establish a shared frame of reference and experiences. This common ground can consist of activities they enjoy, inside jokes, shared challenges, and mutual goals. These experiences help build a narrative of the relationship that both partners can relate to and cherish. Whether it's going for walks, cooking meals together, watching movies, taking trips, or just having consistent open vulnerable conversations, these shared activities deepen the bond and create a positive, loving feeling between them. Regularly spending time together demonstrates that each partner values and prioritizes the relationship, reinforcing their commitment to one another.

Spending time together fosters a sense of closeness that is difficult to replicate in any other way. It is in these moments that partners can engage in meaningful conversations, share laughter, and express affection. These interactions build understanding, familiarity and comfort, which are essential for emotional security and trust. The more time partners spend together, the more they understand each other's personalities, habits, and nuances. This understanding can lead to greater empathy and patience, creating a safer space for both individuals to express themselves freely.

Time spent together also provides opportunities for fun, laughter, and the creation of cherished memories. Enjoying life together helps to alleviate the stresses that naturally arise in any relationship. When partners engage in activities that bring joy and excitement, it strengthens their bond and adds an element of playfulness that keeps the relationship vibrant. These moments of happiness contribute to a positive emotional bank that partners can draw on during times of conflict or hardship. Shared laughter and joyful memories remind partners of the good times and reinforce their desire to stay connected and supportive of one another.

Additionally, spending quality time together has the unique benefit of creating exclusivity within the relationship. It sets the partnership apart from other connections and interactions. This exclusivity is essential for building trust and fostering a sense of security. When partners know that they are making time for each other and that these moments are a priority, it reinforces the idea that their relationship is special and worthy of dedicated attention.

This level of focus fosters a deeper sense of belonging and reassurance, which is vital for sustaining intimacy.

Partners who regularly spend time together also develop a greater impact on one another's lives. The shared experiences and continuous interaction create a lasting impression that shapes their emotional and mental connection. This presence helps partners feel seen, valued, and appreciated. It ensures that their lives are intertwined, with each person playing an active role in the other's daily routine, aspirations, and emotional well-being. This involvement enhances the depth of the relationship and strengthens their ability to rely on each other for support and companionship.

Quality time doesn't have to be extravagant or involve elaborate activities. Sometimes, it's the simplest moments that matter the most—sharing a meal, having a quiet conversation, or sitting in comfortable silence. What's important is that these moments are intentional and meaningful. Prioritizing time together means choosing to be present and engaged, free from distractions like work or technology. This mindfulness in shared moments builds a deeper connection and ensures that both partners feel valued.

Moreover, spending time together not only creates closeness but also fosters emotional and physical intimacy. The more partners interact and share their lives, the more they open up to each other. This openness builds a level of intimacy that goes beyond physical attraction and delves into a deep emotional connection. Partners who consistently make time for each other tend to be more in tune with each other's needs and desires, which strengthens their bond and enhances their love life. The shared time spent helps build anticipation, trust, and affection, making the intimate moments more meaningful and exclusive.

In summary, while many qualities are essential for building and maintaining an intimate relationship, spending time together stands out as the most critical. It is through shared experiences and moments that partners develop a closeness that cannot be achieved through any other means. The more time spent together, the more opportunities there are for fun, laughter, and cherished memories, which in turn solidify the emotional connection. This closeness leads to a relationship marked by exclusivity, understanding, and mutual impact. Ultimately, prioritizing time together ensures that partners stay connected and maintain a strong, loving bond that can weather any challenge life may bring.

I know the question everyone is thinking, what can sustain this type of intimacy? The secret is the glue of patience and forgiveness.

Chapter 18
FORGIVENESS
A Union Without Division Requires Forgiveness

Most of us don't realize the importance and weight that forgiveness has on a person and any relationship. A Godly book that does not mention forgiveness shouldn't be really worthy to claim to be a representation of Godly ways. Is that just me talking? Let's keep going..

Intimacy in a relationship is fragile and can be torn down in moments if it is not rooted in an environment where forgiveness thrives. Though often underestimated and overlooked, forgiveness is essential to the emotional health of individuals and the strength of their relationships. Without it, even the deepest bonds can be eroded by resentment, frustration, and anger. The ability to forgive—truly and consistently—stands out as an unparalleled quality because its absence can have damaging consequences unlike any other.

Forgiveness is necessary for building and maintaining a healthy, close-knit, intimate relationship. Every relationship, no matter how strong or loving, will face challenges, misunderstandings, and mistakes. Human nature makes us susceptible to missteps, whether through harsh words, neglectful actions, or moments of insensitivity. Without forgiveness, these moments can accumulate and breed tension, animosity, and blame. Over time, the lack of forgiveness fosters resentment and frustration, leading to emotional disconnection. The negative emotions that stem from unresolved issues can grow like cancer, contaminating every aspect of the relationship.

The value of forgiveness is immense because it has the power to release partners from the destructive cycle of negativity. When a couple regularly practices forgiveness, it creates an atmosphere of compassion and understanding. This environment encourages vulnerability, where both partners feel safe to admit their faults, knowing that they will be met with empathy and patience. A forgiving spirit breaks down walls of defensiveness and blame, preventing toxic emotions from taking root. As a result, communication improves, trust is rebuilt, and emotional intimacy is reinforced. The act of forgiving not only benefits the person receiving it but also the person giving it. It frees both individuals from carrying the burden of past mistakes and allows them to move forward with a renewed sense of closeness and love.

The power of forgiveness lies in its ability to neutralize the poison of negative emotions. When forgiveness becomes a regular practice, it interrupts the cycle of anger and resentment. A relationship where forgiveness is present is marked by resilience; it can weather conflicts and come out stronger on the other side. This resilience is especially important when handling difficult situations that would otherwise threaten to dismantle intimacy and trust. Forgiveness allows partners to learn from mistakes and grow, turning potentially relationship-ending conflicts into opportunities for deeper connection.

One of the most overlooked aspects of forgiveness is the necessity of forgiving oneself. Self-forgiveness is vital because the inability to release guilt and shame can spill over into the relationship, contaminating it. When a person holds onto self-blame or refuses to forgive themselves, it often manifests as insecurity, self-sabotage, or withdrawal. This self-inflicted negativity can create barriers between partners, leading to misunderstandings and emotional distance. However, when individuals learn to forgive themselves, it opens the door for healing, personal growth, and healthier interactions. Self-forgiveness helps maintain an emotional balance, enabling partners to show up in the relationship with confidence and self-assurance.

True forgiveness is not a one-time act; it is a philosophy that one adopts and lives by. It is a mindset that goes beyond individual moments of conflict and becomes a fundamental part of the relationship's foundation. The willingness to forgive stems from a desire to preserve the bond and emotional well-being of both partners.

It is a mindset that is not only for the other person's sake but for one's own peace and the health of the relationship. The act of forgiving communicates love, commitment to let go, and a belief in the person regardless of the act.

Forgiveness should be a pillar in the life of anyone seeking a Godly and loving relationship. Many religious teachings, including Christian principles, emphasize that forgiveness is non-negotiable and should be practiced without compromise. The Bible, for instance, highlights forgiveness as a divine quality, with verses like Ephesians 4:32: "Be kind and compassionate to one another, forgiving each other, just as in Christ God forgave you." This reflects the idea that just as we are forgiven, we should extend that same grace to others. Embracing forgiveness as a core value aligns a person's actions with love, compassion, and humility, making it an essential quality for a relationship that seeks to mirror divine principles.

Ultimately, forgiveness stands alone in its unmatched power to heal and sustain a relationship. It prevents negative emotions from accumulating, protects intimacy from being eroded, and fosters an environment where love can grow without the chains of past mistakes. Without forgiveness, even the strongest relationships can fall apart under the weight of unresolved grievances. However, when forgiveness is practiced consistently, it ensures that the bond between partners remains strong, resilient, and capable of enduring life's inevitable challenges.

In a union without division, where two individuals share a bond that feels unbreakable, both partners act not as two separate entities, but as one. Every experience, every memory, and every challenge is shared, binding them even more. Such a marriage becomes a source of strength, not strain. Through a foundation of honesty, faithfulness, intimacy, and an understanding of each other's natures, this relationship creates harmony that keeps division and discord at bay. It is, in essence, a "Godly Marriage"—a relationship reflecting deep, unconditional love and spiritual maturity. Fosters forgiveness as a pillar of these fundamentals as a union that strengthens and unifies a marriage without division.

In this next chapter let's discuss some of the subtle differences between men and women that matter. Just to add more opportunities to make a union without division flourish.

Chapter 19
Subtle Differences of Men and Women
Why We Need to Know?

Men and women share many similarities as human beings, but the subtle differences in biology, psyche, and socialization influence how they think, feel, and behave in nearly every aspect of life. These distinctions, while not universal, often shape our interactions, communication, and decision-making in profound ways.

Biological Differences

At a biological level, men and women differ in hormonal makeup and brain structure, which can influence communication and behavior. Testosterone, more prevalent in men, is associated with aggression, competitiveness, and risk-taking. In contrast, women have higher levels of estrogen and oxytocin, hormones linked to nurturing, bonding, and emotional sensitivity. These hormonal differences can shape how men and women approach relationships, solve problems, and express emotions. For instance, women may place a higher emphasis on emotional connection, while men might prioritize action-oriented solutions.

Psychological Differences: Shame, Fear, and Guilt

Men and women often experience shame, fear, and guilt differently due to societal expectations and internalized beliefs. Women may feel shame more acutely when they perceive themselves as failing as caregivers or communicators, given the societal emphasis on empathy and relational skills for women. Men, on the other hand, often feel shame when they perceive a failure in strength, competence, or independence, as traditional masculinity values these traits.

Fear and guilt also manifest differently. Women may experience fear more frequently in social and physical contexts due to safety concerns and societal vulnerabilities, whereas men often suppress fear, as vulnerability is sometimes seen as a weakness. Guilt in women often relates to interpersonal relationships, such as not meeting the needs of others, while in men, it might stem from failing to fulfill societal or career expectations.

Social Influences and Daily Life

Social conditioning deeply influences how men and women interact with the world. Women, often encouraged to be empathetic and cooperative, might excel in collaborative environments but may also feel pressured to prioritize others over themselves. Men, taught to be assertive and self-reliant, might focus on individual achievement but struggle with emotional expression or seeking help. These influences shape not only personal relationships but also professional dynamics and societal roles.

Differences in Choosing Partners

When it comes to relationships, men and women often prioritize different qualities based on biological and social factors. Men might be more influenced by physical attraction and youth, which are subconsciously tied to the motivations of the eyes and the biological drive of men as well as the reproductive health of women. Women often prioritize emotional connection, stability, and long-term potential, reflecting an evolutionary tendency to seek partners who can provide security and long-term emotional support.

Motivations for being in relationships also vary. Men may seek companionship, physical intimacy, and a sense of legacy or relationship in achieving life goals. Women often seek emotional intimacy, shared values, and the fulfillment of relational and nurturing romance feelings and the traditional role of men. These motivations are influenced by both individual desires and cultural narratives.

Understanding these differences can foster greater empathy and cooperation between men and women. While biology and socialization shape distinct tendencies, personal experiences and individuality ultimately define how we connect and grow in relationships. Recognizing and respecting these nuances can enhance communication and strengthen relationships.

One of the fears most of us face is the fear of ending up alone. This may face many in marriage and those wanting marriage.

Chapter 20
Fear of Ending Up Alone
Why Do We Think This?

Many marriages today are forged on the fear of ending up alone, a deep-seated anxiety that drives individuals to pursue and stay in relationships at any cost. This fear stems from societal pressures, personal insecurities, and the pervasive belief that one's happiness is contingent upon another person's presence. Consequently, many people adopt unhealthy habits and behaviors that propel them toward ill-suited marriages.

The fear of loneliness often becomes so overwhelming that individuals feel compelled to settle for partners who may not align with their values or behaviors. They may ignore red flags, suppress their own needs, or rush into relationships without fully understanding themselves or their partner. This is often fueled by a societal narrative that equates marriage with personal fulfillment and success, leading people to prioritize obtaining the "ring" over cultivating a healthy, lasting connection.

Many people believe that their happiness is dependent on finding their "other half," a notion that can lead to a singular focus on finding a partner rather than building a fulfilling life of servitude committed to God's work here on earth. This mindset often results in unhealthy relationship dynamics, where individuals place excessive pressure on their partners to meet all their emotional needs. This dependency can create a fragile foundation, as it neglects the importance of self-awareness, personal growth, and mutual respect.

Furthermore, marriages are frequently forged without a true understanding of the other person. Intense chemistry and attraction can create a false sense of compatibility and beliefs, leading people to commit before they've truly assessed whether their values, goals, lifestyles and God's will align. The excitement of a strong initial connection often overshadows deeper incompatibilities, which can become apparent only after the relationship is formalized.

Having low self-esteem and feelings of inadequacy also play a significant role in driving individuals toward marriage. This is not the forging of a union without division. Also, people who struggle with self-worth may feel that their value is validated only by being chosen by someone else. This can result in a willingness to choose poorly without nurturing or supporting tools for this relationship. For others, a lack of coping skills—often stemming from not being raised in a supportive or emotionally stable environment—leads them to seek comfort and stability through marriage. They view it as a "resting place," an escape from their internal struggles, rather than as a partnership that requires ongoing effort and growth.

Lastly, a profound sense of loneliness can make the idea of being alone feel unbearable. For some, this loneliness becomes the driving force behind their decisions to marry, often leading to unions that are built on unhealthy dependency rather than mutual alignment, compatibility, respect and love. When individuals believe they cannot survive on their own, they may tolerate unhealthy or even toxic relationships, viewing them as preferable to solitude.

These dynamics reveal the importance of addressing one's fears, insecurities, and societal conditioning before entering into a life-long commitment. Healthy marriages are built on self-awareness, mutual respect, and emotional and spiritual maturity—not on the fear of being alone. Recognizing and addressing these underlying issues can empower individuals to seek relationships that are genuinely fulfilling, rather than settling for those born of fear or desperation.

Does God Commission us to marry

Many believe marriage offers benefits that enhance a person's life emotionally, socially, and even spiritually. And for many marriages it does. However, it's important to note that marriage isn't automatically better for everyone. A healthy, loving person (married or not) is better than a toxic or forced marriage. Many may believe that marriage is a commission from God. Marriage is both a choice and a divine invitation but not a universal command. God gives people free will. In Scripture, people choose whether or not to marry. Paul even says in 1 Corinthians 7 that singleness is honorable and can allow for undivided devotion to God. God often calls people into marriage as a sacred relationship to honor God. This is because sexual relationships without the covering of marriage is sin. It reflects the covenant between Christ and the Church (Ephesians 5:25–33). For many, who chose it to be a part of their life's purpose and ministry—to serve and grow with another person. Marriage is not a one-size-fits-all calling nor is it intended to be a filler not to be lonely or all along. God doesn't require everyone to marry. Jesus and Paul were single, and both spoke highly of the single life when lived with purpose. What matters most is obedience to God's calling—whether that includes marriage or not. People often believe marriage makes life better because of the emotional, social, and spiritual benefits it can offer. Marriage is a choice to honor God with a partner in life, that God honors, and for some, who believe it's a divine commission within their spiritual walk. But marriage is not a union just to benefit us or satisfy us emotionally, socially, or a commandment.

In conclusion let us be careful and consider not to let being married or getting married and the fear of ending up alone be the reason. Don't allow your fears to pursue or maintain marriage at any cost. Position yourself with marriage as a testament to glorify God without societal pressures, personal insecurities, and the pervasive belief that one's happiness is contingent upon another person's presence. Consequently, consider God first and place God first in your marriage.

CHAPTER 21
LIVING WITH UNREASONABLE KINDNESS, GRACE, AND UN-CONDITIONAL LOVE

God's Love God's Way

Imagine being in a relationship with someone who treats you with an overwhelming amount of kindness and care, the kind that feels almost undeserved. Their kindness is not transactional—it doesn't depend on how you behave, what you do, or how well you perform. It simply flows, steady and unwavering, as if it were an endless river. Even when you make mistakes or hurt them, they respond with grace so quickly that it leaves you speechless. You've barely had time to feel guilty before they've already forgiven you—not begrudgingly, not with a reminder of the pain, but as if it never happened.

In this kind of relationship, you find yourself standing on sacred ground. Mistakes that would typically cause arguments or resentment somehow become insignificant because they don't keep score. There is no mental ledger keeping track of who has hurt whom or who owes what. It is almost unsettling at first—this radical grace—because we are so accustomed to people remembering every hurt, nursing old wounds, and using past offenses to justify present anger. But this person doesn't dwell on pain. They release it into thin air, as if it has no weight in their heart. You may find yourself asking, "How can they be so forgiving?" But before you can wrap your mind around it, they've moved on—not just outwardly, but inwardly, with no trace of bitterness left behind.

Living with someone who forgives instantly, without strings attached, changes you in profound ways. There is no debt in this relationship. When they forgive, it isn't stored up as ammunition to use later. It's not a transaction where kindness today demands kindness tomorrow. Instead, their grace is given freely, and when they let go of something, it stays gone—vanished from both memory and heart. There is no keeping score because, for them, love doesn't function that way. They don't expect perfection from you, nor do they require that you earn their affection. They simply love, and they love well.

This experience is transformative. At first, you might be tempted to test the limits, as if to see whether their kindness has a breaking point. But each time, you are met with the same compassion, the same gentle forgiveness. There are no angry outbursts, no icy silences, no emotional punishments to make you feel the weight of your wrongs. Instead, you are given space to be human—space to fail, to learn, and to grow without fear of rejection or condemnation.

It is humbling to live with someone whose humility is so profound that it changes the way you see yourself. Their gentleness feels like a mirror, reflecting both the best and the worst in you, but without shame or judgment. In their presence, you become acutely aware of your flaws—not because they point them out, but because their kindness compels you to want to be better. Their grace doesn't enable bad behavior; instead, it inspires you to rise above it. You find yourself striving to match their love, even though deep down you know that you never fully can. But the beauty of it is that they don't expect you to.

Living with someone who gives without limits—without expecting anything in return—feels like encountering a rare kind of freedom. There is no pressure to perform, no burden of proving your worth. They give generously of their time, their energy, and their love, pouring into you without hesitation. And even when life gets messy, even when you are at your lowest, they are there—steadfast, patient, and compassionate. Their love is not conditional on how good or strong you are; it flows even when you are weak, tired, or broken.

The weight of such love can be overwhelming, not in a burdensome way but in a way that makes you feel indebted—not because they expect repayment, but because you are aware that nothing you do could ever equal the depth of their love. It's the kind of love that makes you want to give more, love better, and live with greater intention—not out of obligation, but out of gratitude. Their humility shines so brightly that it pulls you toward becoming a better version of yourself, not through force but through quiet influence.

Their empathy is not superficial; it runs deep and is woven into everything they do. They anticipate your needs before you even voice them and respond to your emotions with a tenderness that is almost hard to believe. Whether you're happy, sad, frustrated, or confused, they meet you exactly where you are without judgment or impatience. They seem to have a gift for knowing how to comfort you in ways that words alone cannot express. Their presence alone is enough to calm storms within you. In their arms, you feel a peace that surpasses understanding—a peace that tells you, "It's okay to be exactly who you are."

Loving someone like this makes you realize that their love is not dependent on who you are in the moment but is rooted in something much deeper—something that transcends circumstances, moods, and mistakes. It's a love that exists in spite of you, in spite of what you say or do. It's a love that stands firm even when you are at your worst. It is as if they have made a decision to love you no matter what, and nothing can alter that decision.

This kind of love teaches you something profound: it shows you that true love is not earned or conditional—it is given freely, even when it's undeserved. And the more you experience this kind of love, the more you realize that you cannot bear to live without it. It becomes a source of life, a wellspring of joy and peace that sustains you through everything. It is a love without bounds—one that stretches farther than you thought possible, reaching into every corner of your life and transforming it from the inside out.

Living with someone like this makes you understand what it truly means to love and be loved. It strips away every misconception about love being a transaction or a reward for good behavior. It reveals love as an endless well, poured out with no expectation of return. And as you receive this kind of love, you find yourself longing to reflect it back—not because you are required to, but because you are compelled to. Their kindness, grace, and compassion have such a profound impact on you that loving them becomes the most natural response in the world.

In the end, being in a relationship with someone like this teaches you that love is not about keeping track or settling scores—it's about giving, forgiving, and growing together. It's about creating a space where both people can flourish, free from the fear of judgment or rejection. It's about choosing grace over resentment, humility over pride, and compassion over control.

And perhaps the greatest lesson of all is this: love like this doesn't just change the one receiving it—it transforms the one giving it too. It creates a bond so deep, so unshakable, that even the hardest moments cannot break it. It becomes a love that you know you could never live without—a love that fills your heart to overflowing and spills out into every area of your life.

This is the kind of love that is rare and precious. It is the kind of love that heals, restores, and redeems. And once you've tasted it, you know that nothing else will ever compare. It is a love un-leashed—a love that knows no limits, keeps no record of wrongs, and offers grace upon grace without end. It is, quite simply, the greatest gift you could ever receive.

A Love Beyond Compare

In every sense, this husband is truly incomparable. His love, patience, and understanding create a relationship that is built to last, a relationship that is both resilient and deeply fulfilling. He is not just a partner; he is a source of strength, a pillar of support, and a trusted friend. His presence brings joy, peace, and purpose to his wife's life, making him irreplaceable.

This kind of love is a gift—a love that is steady, patient, and root-ed in a deep understanding of each other's hearts. In him, she finds not only a husband but a true partner in every sense. Her life is richer, her heart fuller, and her love deeper because of the man he is. His love is not only a blessing; it is a rare and precious gift, a love that she cherishes every day. Okay, living with this type of unreasonable kindness, grace, and unconditional love—only leads us to a union without division.

Chapter 22
Conclusion
A Love — A Union
A Promise — Without Divi-
sion

A Union Without Division (recap)

In a union without division, where two individuals share a bond that just feels unbreakable, is truly about a marriage to please God. A union like this one, both partners believes, understands, and acts not as two separate entities, but as one. Every bonding experience, every cherished memory, and every individual challenge is shared, even when they stand as one they stand together.

For example, If one partner was a journalist and had to make a choice to report on a story for the sake of journalism that can damage or separate the structure of their family, and this partner is committed to their career and integrity—they wouldn't make that decision without the other's confirmation and agreement to do so. In a union without division there are two choices with one decision to honor and appreciate one another, a commitment that is binding not because but despite. Such a marriage becomes a source of strength, not strain. Such a marriage becomes an effortless desire, not work. The center of this strength is its compatibility through surrender and submission. Through a foundation of honesty, faithfulness, intimacy, and an understanding of each other's natures, this relationship creates harmony that keeps division and discord at bay. It is, in essence, a "Godly Marriage"—a relationship reflecting deep, unconditional love and spiritual maturity. For instance, these fundamental steps that strengthen and unify a marriage without division:

1. Honesty: A Relationship Founded on Honesty that Inspires Transparency

In this marriage, honesty is more than just being truthful in a surface-level sense; it's about inviting full transparency. Honesty in this context doesn't merely answer questions; it anticipates potential concerns and shares openly before misunderstandings can arise. Transparency removes ambiguity and secrecy, allowing trust to deepen. For instance, if a husband runs into an ex-partner by chance, he shares this encounter with his spouse, not out of obligation but to ensure clarity and trust. This honesty helps protect both partners from hurt or confusion that might arise from situations left unspoken.

With full transparency, cracks that might otherwise widen into the difference of these two are quickly sealed. Small acts of secrecy, even those that seem inconsequential, can otherwise build up, leading each partner to cultivate private lives or relationships outside the marriage. Honest communication also nurtures an environment where both partners feel secure, knowing they are genuinely aware of each other's lives and emotions. This honesty provides a shield, protecting the marriage from divisive secrets that can erode its foundation.

2. Faithfulness: A Commitment to Loyalty and Integrity In Self
Faithfulness in a union without division is not circumstantial but a defining characteristic of each individual. This kind of faithfulness isn't conditional on how one's partner behaves or responds. Instead, each partner chooses loyalty as a personal standard and sticks to it unconditionally. Faithfulness becomes an act of self-respect as much as respect for the partner, creating a solid foundation for trust.

When faithfulness is deeply embedded in the character of both partners, the relationship is safeguarded from the destructive tendencies of infidelity, both physical and emotional. Here, commitment goes beyond marital vows; it becomes a daily choice. This commitment to loyalty becomes an anchor, holding the couple steady regardless of external temptations or life's challenges. Through such unwavering faithfulness, both partners experience peace and stability, eliminating the anxieties that distrust can introduce.

3. Intimacy: A Spiritual and Emotional Connection Beyond the Physical

This type of Intimacy unifies marriage that transcends physical attraction and chemistry; it is rooted in a spiritual and principles to glorify God. This form of intimacy acknowledges physical connection as essential, but it does not rely on it as the sole form of closeness. Rather, intimacy here is expressed through compassionate service, mutual support, mutual understanding, and shared purpose. When passion inevitably fluctuates, this marriage remains anchored by the deeper love and commitment that goes beyond physical attraction.

Such intimacy ensures that both partners feel connected despite the demands of family life, careers, outside influences, and life changes. In times when responsibilities pile up—raising children, caring for aging parents, or managing busy careers—the couple can still lean on each other, finding solace and strength in their bond. Because intimacy is continually nurtured through acts of service, a deep understanding of one another, and kindness, it cannot become stale or routine. It is a commitment to each other's emotional, physical, and spiritual needs, which ensures that they never feel like mere roommates, a new sense of codependents.

4. Understanding Male and Female Natures: Embracing Differences

A union without division recognizes and honors the unique nature of each partner. Understanding the fundamental differences in male and female nature, and perspectives allows for empathy and respect, reducing misunderstandings and frustration. This marriage prioritizes knowing and honoring how each partner thinks, communicates, and processes emotions. This understanding is seeded in patience.

When both partners have this understanding, they communicate more effectively and avoid the pitfalls of projection or assumption. Rather than assuming that their partner will respond as they would, they take time to consider each other's unique position and needs. This empathy and understanding can be transformative, eliminating many common conflicts and misunderstandings that lead to discord in relationships. When differences are seen as complementary strengths rather than sources of division, they enrich the marriage and bring balance.

Additional Principles That Reinforce a Union Without Division

Consistent Communication: Open, thoughtful communication is essential. Rather than bottling up feelings, both partners share their thoughts, dreams, concerns, and desires. Especially when times are difficult. They address concerns before they fester and make a habit of communicating without accusations or blame.

A God Forgiveness: Mistakes and misunderstandings are inevitable, but this marriage thrives on quick and sincere forgiveness. Each partner understands that holding onto grudges weakens their bond, so they choose to release negative emotions for the sake of unity. Practice and patience of letting go..

Mutual Respect: Respect is woven into every action and word. By respecting each other's opinions, dreams, and individuality, the couple ensures that they grow together, not apart.

Shared Values and Goals: A shared vision for the future brings them together with purpose and direction. Whether it's family goals, financial plans, or personal growth, they move in alignment, fostering a partnership that is purpose-driven.

Sacrifice and Servitude: Each partner is willing to sacrifice for the other's happiness and well-being. This willingness to serve each other fosters a profound sense of love, as each partner sees that the other is committed to their shared joy.

Conclusion

A marriage without division requires work on yourself—not the relationship. It requires honest intention, and a commitment to principles that safeguard and strengthen the relationship, God's way. By building a foundation on honesty, faithfulness, intimacy, and mutual understanding, this union remains resilient and deeply satisfying. Each partner's commitment to positive patterns—whether through transparency, empathy, forgiveness, or shared values—reinforces their bond, allowing them to thrive in unity.

In the end, such a marriage stands as a testament to what two individuals can achieve when they are devoted not just to each other but to God's idea of harmony, growth, and a lifelong partnership within a relationship of marriage. This kind of union reflects a love that is not only romantic but rooted in the highest ideals of compassion, commitment, and grace. It is a marriage not merely of two people but of two souls intertwined in purpose and shared vision, leading to a union that truly has no division—A union without division.

Chapter 23
Bonus Chapter
Communication
Recommendations
Clarify with I, Edify with You

Many enter godly marriage believing it is primarily a self-fulfilling partnership—an emotional, financial, and physical union meant to meet personal needs. But this misunderstanding often sets couples up for unmet expectations and eventual frustration and eventually divorce. When we lose sight of the true purpose of marriage, we risk treating it as a contract rather than a covenant. In the end, such a marriage stands as a testament to what two individuals can achieve when they are devoted not just to each other but to God's idea of harmony, growth, and lifelong partners within a relationship of marriage.

Marriage was never meant to be centered around personal gain or personal desires. It is a sacred covenant, divinely ordained by God, designed to glorify Him. At its core, marriage is meant to model the relationship between Christ and His Church—a relationship marked by love, sacrifice, grace, and truth. When we approach marriage with this understanding, it transforms how we view our spouse, ourselves, and the way we communicate.

This chapter is especially for those who have awakened to the reality of a marriage marked by frustration, disconnection, or disappointment. Also, the many who believe that they truly can't communicate with their partner. If you find yourself wondering how things became so difficult—or if restoration is even possible—know this: healing often begins with awareness and you, and with understanding and with healthier communication.``1

I write this chapter because many if not most believe that relationships are heavily based on communication. So let's dive into some helpful communication tips.

Below are practical, grace-filled recommendations for building better communication in your marriage. These are not quick fixes, but intentional steps you can begin taking to rebuild trust, foster understanding, and make room for restoration. Whether your marriage feels wounded or just weary, these principles can help you create space for a more God-centered, life-giving connection.

Let's begin a new journey to connect and reconnect—one honest, humble, and healing conversation at a time.

Recommendations for Healthy Communication in Marriage

1. Commit to Listening Before Speaking

True communication begins with listening—not just to words, but to your spouse's nature, experiences, and past. This is listening to their intentions behind the words. What that means is you listen by understanding their experiences and past relationships. Listen with empathy, not defensiveness, listen with the intent to help, support, and influence, not to change, blame or control. Make space for your spouse to feel heard, valued, and understood.

2. Speak the Truth in Love and Kindness

Honesty is essential, but it should be partnered with patience, grace and transparency. Share your thoughts and feelings truthfully, but do so with kindness and patience, aiming to build up rather than tear down (Ephesians 4:15). The truth without gentleness is the truth without the presence of God. It does matter how we tell the truth.

3. Pray Before You Process

Before entering hard conversations, take time to pray—individually and then together. Ask the Holy Spirit to guide your thoughts and words, calm your emotions, and help you see each other through God's eyes. Pray that you receive understanding of the other person's perspective. Take time to self reflect and when and where to pause when having difficult conversations.

4. Use "I" Statements Instead of You or Blame

Say, "I feel hurt when…" rather than, "You always…" This approach avoids accusations and invites your spouse into a conversation rather than a conflict.

5. Create Safe Spaces for Vulnerability

Foster a home environment where it's safe to express weaknesses, disappointments, or needs without fear of ridicule or judgment. This should be an actual space in your home set aside. This space should be set aside for difficult conversations and agreed it's for no arguing, complaining, accusing, criticising, or judging. This space and time is for helping one another to understand the concerns, support, and influence, not to change, blame or control. This builds trust and emotional intimacy. This Safe Space also invites growth both together and individually.

6. Avoid Speaking in Absolutes

Phrases like "You never…" or "You always…" exaggerate the issue and put your spouse on the defensive. Stick to specific examples and focus on finding solutions. There may be times to just let each other be heard. There are times to just let it go (refer to the chapter Forgiveness).

7. Stay Present—Mentally and Emotionally

Give your spouse your full attention. Practice active listening, such as periodically repeating some of the things they are saying, asking questions about their concerns, giving affirmations, paying attention and paying attention to nonverbal cues, and providing feedback if requested. Put away distractions, maintain eye contact, and resist the urge to rehearse your response while they're speaking.

8. Be Quick to Apologize and Forgive

This is my favorite. Practice this daily. Humility partnered with grace is the gateway to peace, joy, healing and strength. Be willing to admit when you're wrong and quick to extend forgiveness. Reconciliation is more important than being right.

9. Check Your Tone and Timing

What you say matters, but *how and when you say it matters much more.* Avoid serious discussions when either of you is tired, angry, or emotionally overwhelmed. Just stop!

10. Invite God into the Conversation

Remember that your marriage belongs to God, not you. Regularly ask Him to help you communicate in ways that reflect His heart, His words. Honor His Word, and serve one another in His love.

Healthy communication is not a one-time fix—it's a lifestyle of humility, grace, and intentionality. Healthy communication requires practice. As you begin to practice these principles, you'll not only improve how you talk with each other, but also strengthen the sacred covenant you share. Through patience, understanding, and prayer, even broken places can be rebuilt.

Reflection Questions

Take time to reflect individually and take time to discuss together:

1. When was the last time I truly listened to my spouse without interrupting or forming a response in my mind?
2. Are there patterns in my communication (tone, timing, language) that may hinder connection?
3. In what ways have I allowed selfish expectations to shape how I relate to my spouse?
4. What is a constructive way to look at the situation and without judging my spouse?
5. How has my behavior been as a contributing factor positively to the conversation or situation?
6. What is one step I can take this week to foster a safer space for honest conversation in our marriage?
7. Have I practiced gratitude toward my spouse this week?
8. Is it as important to understand the issue as it is to consider my feelings?
9. Would God be pleased with my attitude and actions toward my spouse?
10. How often do we invite God into our communication—and how can we do that more intentionally?

Have a certain prayer when dealing with conflict with your spouse (example)

Father God,

Thank You for the gift of marriage. Thank You for creating it not just for our joy, but for Your glory. We confess that we have not always spoken to each other in love, nor have we always listened with compassion. Forgive us for the words that have wounded, the silence that has distanced, and the pride that has built walls.

Lord, teach us how to communicate with humility and grace. Help us to reflect the heart of Christ in how we speak, listen, and respond. Fill our hearts with patience, our minds with understanding, and our mouths with words that build, not break. Let Your Spirit be the guide of every conversation.

Restore what has been broken. Heal what has been bruised. Reignite what has grown cold. Make our marriage a sanctuary where Your presence dwells and Your love is made known. May our communication not only strengthen our bond but also honor You in every way. In Jesus' name, **Amen.**

When it comes to difficult conversations, many people fall into the trap of passive communication. Even worse, no communication. This happens when someone avoids expressing what's really on their mind. Instead of speaking up, they hold it in—often hoping the other person will just "pick up on it." But the truth is, no one can read our minds. When we don't share our thoughts or concerns clearly, our needs remain unmet, and over time, invisible walls begin to form in the relationship.

Passive communicators tend to quietly accept the other person's position, even when they disagree. At first this might seem easier, but over time, it creates an unhealthy pattern where one person's voice dominates while the other retreats. This can breed fear, shame, or a deep desire to avoid conflict altogether.

On the other hand, some people swing to the opposite extreme: aggressive communication. This style feels dominating—it comes across as blaming, attacking, finger-pointing, or judging. While it may get immediate attention, it damages trust and pushes people away rather than bringing them closer.

The healthiest approach is assertive communication. Assertiveness means being direct, but also respectful. It means speaking with confidence, but carrying humility. It's about expressing your needs, feelings, and thoughts with honesty and clarity—while keeping compassion at the center. Assertive communication also requires timeliness: don't bottle things up until they turn into frustration or anger. Address matters openly and calmly before they grow into bigger issues.

When we practice assertive communication with a godly mindset—grounded in humility, empathy, and understanding—we create space for acceptance, patience and forgiveness. This kind of communication invites connection rather than conflict, and builds trust rather than tearing it down.

Chapter 24
Benediction
Faith, Love, & Shared Purpose

Faith in a godly marriage means placing complete trust in Jesus Christ and the Kingdom of God above our own understanding. Love in a godly marriage means learning God's ways and loving Him with all our heart, soul, and mind through your marriage. Shared purpose in a godly marriage means choosing a life partner who shares this same faith, mission, vision and purpose as you do. This is the vision of *a union without division.*

This is not just an idea, but a call—a call for all believers in Christ to walk in unity, humility, and service within marriage. Do this within your marriage before you face the world.

Imagine a marriage where self-interest yields to the well-being of the union. God's union. A union rooted in love, shaped by the example of Christ, marked by servanthood and sacrifice.

A union without division thrives in compassion and joy, being like-minded, of one spirit, and of one mind. It is not mere outward agreement but inward unity, born of shared love that reflects the very heart of Christ. This unity imitates His humility, doing nothing out of selfish ambition or vain conceit, but valuing one another above self. This is not equality in worldly terms, but mutual service in God's design—husband and wife living in obedience, compassion, and humility, placing the other before self with joy.

Such a union becomes a witness to the world. It demonstrates humility and unity, in a culture built on pride, compromise, and division. It refuses the lure of envy, competition, and self-gratification, instead showing that true marriage is rooted in God's design, not man's ideas.

A union without division embraces joy—not the fragile joy of circumstances, but the supernatural joy of Christ. It is joy that endures in trials, that shines in suffering, that sees hardships as opportunities for God's glory. Like the Apostle Paul, such a marriage lives by the words, *"To live is Christ, and to die is gain."* This perspective is not natural; it is Spirit-born—Supernatural. It trusts God's promises, rejoices in His presence, and stands unshaken by life's storms.

This union reflects the truth that every part of life must be aligned with Christ. It points others to Him, reminding the world that sufficiency, hope, and purpose are found in Jesus alone. It bears fruit in faith, love, and thanksgiving, spreading the Gospel through its witness.

In a world full of false teachings and distorted views of marriage, a union without division is anchored in the Word of God. It is built not on shifting sand on man but on the solid rock of Christ. It displays love as the thread weaving together compassion, patience, humility, and peace—the peace of Christ reigning in grateful hearts. In such a union, wives submit to their husbands without contest as unto the Lord, and husbands love their wives in spite of any challenges with Christlike tenderness, never in harshness but in sacrificial love. This is not hierarchy but harmony, this is not compromise but spiritual compatibility, a reflection of Christ's love for His church.

A union without division is a lifestyle of prayer, watchfulness, and thanksgiving. It is steadfast, disciplined, and discerning in a world that does not share its values and doesn't understand its ways. Its words and actions are always seasoned with grace and love, shining as a light that draws others to Christ.

Such a marriage is not about wealth or status but about strength in reliance on Christ, based on servitude and surrender. It invites both husband and wife to pour into one another, to sow seeds of hope, and to partner in God's mission. Through generosity, humility, and spiritual unity—their lives ripple outward as a living testimony of God's love.

And so, we close with this charge: guard the Gospel in your life and in your marriage. Do not blend God's truth with the world's counterfeit. Marriage is not man's invention; it is God's holy design, birthed by His Spirit from the beginning. To neglect this truth is to build on sand, but to embrace it is to build on the immovable rock of Christ.

The question remains: Is Scripture shaping your marriage? Are you letting it transform your thoughts and guide your actions, or is it gathering dust while the world shapes your view of love, marriage, and commitment?

Let us lay aside pride, ambition, self-gratification and the need to be right for the sake of loving one another as Christ loved us. For a marriage rooted in Christ is more than companionship—it is a testimony of God's Kingdom and His Glory—on earth just like it is in heaven.

Glossary
Bible Verses To Strengthen Your Marriage

Foundation

Genesis 2:24

A man shall leave his father and mother and hold fast to his wife, and they shall become one flesh.

Lesson: Marriage requires leaving, cleaving, and uniting — forming a new family.

Reflection: Have we fully prioritized our marriage above other relationships?

Matthew 19:6

So they are no longer two but one flesh. What therefore God has joined together, let not man separate.

Lesson: Marriage requires shared belief, purpose, & body — A lifestyle of harmony, one in mind and in body.

Reflection: Do we invest a majority of our time and interest together? Have we fully considered the benefits and consequences of sanctifying our body? Do we follow God's plans for marriage or our own?

Matthew 22:37-38

Jesus states."Love the Lord your God with all your heart and with all your soul and with all your mind. This is the first and greatest commandment." He further clarifies this by saying the greatest commandment is to love God with everything you are, encompassing your deep affections, your entire being, and all your thoughts

Lesson: As individuals and in marriage God requires that He comes first. This means His love, His thoughts, His behavior, and all His ways in your marriage and not yours. — A life, a marriage connected with harmony with God. —The only way to One Flesh **Reflection:** Do we honestly seek God first in our marriages, invest a godly mindset to all our ups and downs? Have we fully prioritized God Love in our marriage?

We could stop here but let's continue..

On Love & Unity

1 Corinthians 13:4–7

Love is patient and kind; love does not envy or boast; it is not arrogant or rude… Love bears all things, believes all things, hopes all things, endures all things.

Lesson: This is the blueprint for godly love. Marriage requires being mindful to always put the other person first especially when times are difficult and challenging. Patience is a learned behavior derived from a practice mindset.

Reflection: Do we practice patience daily? Marriage needs us not to criticize or place judgment on our spouse—How does this show up in our marriage? How do I acquire these qualities to grow? Start practicing self-awareness. Every time you catch yourself not being patient with anyone, stop, time to reflect it's not about you.

1 Peter 4:8

Above all, keep loving one another earnestly, since love covers a multitude of sins.

Lesson: Marriage is about choices not feelings. These choices create feelings but it's the choices that sustain our marriages not our feelings. To love your spouse as God intents is to keep choosing God first. To put them first is to put God first.

Reflection: Do we choose to love our partner when they don't deserve it? Do we make it easy to be loved?

1 Ephesians 5:25

Husbands, love your wives, as Christ loved the church and gave himself up for her.

Lesson: For husbands who have chosen marriage your responsibility is to love your wife in, through, and past all her irritations, inconveniences, and shortcomings because that is the commitment you made to God as your sacrifice.

Reflection: Do you put your wife first no matter what? In every decision you make do you consider your wife first? Do you know your wife is your responsibility? Do you give yourself up for her? Do you love your wife like Christ loved the church? *Stop making excuses..*

1 Ephesians 5:33

However, let each one of you love his wife as himself, and let the wife see that she respects her husband.

Lesson: For husbands, show your wife at any and every opportunity how you put her first. Treat her as the best part of your body and the favorite part of your thoughts and the deepest parts of your feelings.

Reflection: Husbands when she sees you are spending more time at your job, with your car, with sports or any of these things that isn't God stop, you are failing.

Marriage Roles & Responsibilities / Submission & Honor

1 Ephesians 5:22-33

Wives submit to your own husbands, as to the Lord... Husbands, love your wives, as Christ loved the church... This mystery is profound, and I am saying that it refers to Christ and the church.

Submitting to one another out of reverence for Christ. For the husband is the head of the wife as Christ is the head of the church, his body, of which he is the Savior. Now as the church submits to Christ, so also wives should submit to their husbands in everything. Husbands, love your wives, just as Christ loved the church and gave himself up for her. To make her holy, cleansing her by the washing with water through the word. And to present her to himself as a radiant church, without stain or wrinkle or any other blemish, but holy and blameless. In this same way, husbands ought to love their wives as their own bodies. He who loves his wife loves himself. After all, no one ever hated their own body, but they feed and care for their body, just as Christ does the church for we are members of his body. "For this reason a man will leave his father and mother and be united to his wife, and the two will become one flesh." This is a profound mystery—but I am talking about Christ and the church. However, each one of you also must love his wife as he loves himself, and the wife must respect her husband.

Colossians 3:18–19

Wives, Wives, submit to your husbands, as is fitting in the Lord. Husbands, love your wives, and do not be harsh with them.

1 Peter 3:7

Likewise, husbands, live with your wives in an understanding way, showing honor to the woman… so that your prayers may not be hindered.

Genesis 2:18

Then the Lord God said, "It is not good that the man should be alone; I will make him a helper fit for him."

Lesson: A husband & a wife is not only a title, they are roles according to the bible. These verses express many things, mostly in a marriage a man and woman is designed to fit into a unit of one. For husbands are the head of the wife because he is responsible for the wife. To love her is to make her holy in God's eyes by using the word as she repents her mind of worldly things. For wives submit everything you have and yours to your husband as it pleases God to do this for a man who seeks God's presence. A godly marriage requires your differences to be submitted under the role of husband and wife. A godly marriage requires roles that are not to be equal. Not equal as male and female, not equal as husband and wife or in any capacity except our soul and our love for God—marriage requires us to put the other first. Marriage becomes the balance when there is mutual love, understanding, respect, and gentleness.

Reflection: Do we show love and respect in a way that reflects Christ? Do I put my spouse first before me?

Forgiveness & Patience

Colossians 3:13

Bearing with one another and forgiving each other; as the Lord has forgiven you, so you also must forgive.

Lesson: Forgiveness restores peace and unity. As individuals and in marriage God requires forgiveness. This means His love, His thoughts, His behavior, and all His ways in your marriage and not yours. — A life, a marriage connected with forgiveness and humility with God.

Reflection: Is there anything I need to forgive or let go of today? Do I let go of the past and give the present of grace? Do we honestly seek God first in our marriages, invest a godly mindset to all our ups and downs? Have we fully prioritized God Love in our marriage?

Kindness & Generosity

Ephesians 4:1–3

Walk in a manner worthy of the calling… with all humility and gentleness, with patience, bearing with one another in love—intimacy that is rooted in love also embraces self-love.

Ephesians 4:2–3

With all humility and gentleness, with patience, bearing with one another in love, eager to maintain the unity of the Spirit in the bond of peace.

Ephesians 4:32

Be kind to one another, tenderhearted, forgiving one another, as God in Christ forgave you.

Lesson: Lesson: Humility and patience create a peaceful home.

Reflection: Where do I need to be more patient or gentle in our marriage?

Conflicts

Colossians 3:13

Bearing with one another and forgiving each other; as the Lord has forgiven you, so you also must forgive.

Lesson: As individuals and in marriage God requires that he comes first. This means His love, His thoughts, His behavior, and all His ways in your marriage and not yours. — A life, a marriage connected with harmony with God.

Reflection: Do we honestly seek God first in our marriages, invest a godly mindset to all our ups and downs? Have we fully prioritized God Love in our marriage?

Infidelity

Hebrews 13:4

Let marriage be held in honor among all, and let the marriage bed be undefiled, for God will judge the sexually immoral and adulterous.

Lesson: Faithfulness and purity protect marriage and bring honor to God.

Reflection: Are we guarding purity and trust in our relationship? Do I surrender my body to her? Do I surrender my body to him?

Ephesians 4:1–3

Walk in a manner worthy of the calling… with all humility and gentleness, with patience, bearing with one another in love—intimacy that is rooted in love also embraces self-love.

Lesson: Marriage is a choice to accept the calling, to live out a Christlike character. Faithfulness and purity protect marriage and bring honor to God.

Reflection: How can I "walk worthy" in my role as husband or wife? What does God want from me for my spouse?

Intimacy

Proverbs 5:17

Let them be yours alone, never to be shared with strangers.

Ephesians 4:1–3

Walk in a manner worthy of the calling… with all humility and gentleness, with patience, bearing with one another in love—intimacy that is rooted in love also embraces self-love.

Ephesians 4:2–3

With all humility and gentleness, with patience, bearing with one another in love, eager to maintain the unity of the Spirit in the bond of peace.

Ephesians 4:32

Be kind to one another, tenderhearted, forgiving one another, as God in Christ forgave you.

Lesson: As we grow and learn patience and generosity forges the bond for intimacy in marriage. An intimacy that is rooted in patience, kindness, compassion, and generosity also embraces self-love. This is the quickest path to intimacy.

Reflection: Do I give more? How can I be more patient? Where do I need to be more patient or gentle in our marriage? Do I out love my spouse?

Blessing of Marriage

Proverbs 18:22

He who finds a wife finds a good thing and obtains favor from the Lord.

Lesson: Marriage is a blessing, not a burden.

Reflection: How can we show more gratitude for one another daily?

Proverbs 31:10

An excellent wife who can find? She is far more precious than jewels.

Lesson: A godly spouse is of immeasurable worth. This verse demonstrates how difficult it may be to find a wife of virtue. If you do value her more precious than jewels.

Reflection: Do you know that to find a wife of virtue is to find the most valuable gift on earth? Do I honor and value my spouse as precious before God?

Hebrews 13:4

Let marriage be held in honor among all, and let the marriage bed be undefiled, for God will judge the sexually immoral and adulterous.

Lesson: Let your marriage honor God first!

Reflection: Do I honor God in and with my marriage?

Remember. A marriage becomes a union without division only when both husband and wife learn to live under the guidance of the Holy Spirit. Spiritual growth within marriage does not begin with behavior modification or conflict resolution techniques—it begins when both individuals invite the Holy Spirit to dwell not only within them, but between them. This invitation is expressed daily through the posture of the heart and the words spoken within the covenant.

Our words have the power to welcome the Holy Spirit into a marriage or to resist His presence. *Be blessed*

We love to hear from you

"A Union Without Division" is a transformative guide to building and sustaining a marriage that is truly undivided. In this groundbreaking book, the author takes readers on a captivating journey from the foundations of an unbreakable union to the enduring beauty of a lifelong commitment. Each chapter unveils a new layer of understanding, offering profound insights into the nature of men and women under a covenant with God, the intricacies of relationships, and the timeless principles that form the cornerstone of an unbreakable bond.

With clarity and compassion, Darrell Canty delves into the essential qualities of a thriving marriage—honesty, transparency, trust, awareness, understanding, and a shared vision of God's design. By examining the roots of division, this book offers practical tools to navigate challenges while fostering connection and mutual growth. Through compelling stories, relatable examples, and actionable advice, the author presents a fresh perspective on the age-old institution of marriage, showing how awareness, understanding, and a clear choice can create a union free from the specter of divorce.

Thank you so much for reading this book; it means the world to me. If you found this book helpful, inspiring, or just enjoyable, Please take a moment and leave a review.

Thank you for your support

Scan Me

www.darrellcanty.net

www.ingramcontent.com/pod-product-compliance
Lightning Source LLC
Chambersburg PA
CBHW070751160726
48004CB00001B/141